FIGHTIN' IRISH

FOR ALL THE BIG NUMBERS AND THE LITTLE-KNOWN FACTS ABOUT NOTRE DAME FOOTBALL, INCLUDING:

- the names of the seven Notre Dame Heisman Trophy winners—more than any other school

- the two Fighting Irish quarterbacks who were ahead of Joe Montana at the beginning of the 1977 national championship season

- the significance of the number 59,075 to the Notre Dame football program

- the university for which Knute Rockne considered leaving Notre Dame . . . and the reason he ultimately remained

- the member of the famed Four Horsemen who later went on to become a Notre Dame coach

- the story behind the "Legend of Harry O," one of the most miraculous plays in Notre Dame history

- and much more!

FIGHTIN' IRISH

The A–Z
Notre Dame Football
Trivia Book

Tony Pace *and* **Mark Spellen**

POCKET BOOKS
New York   London   Toronto   Sydney   Tokyo   Singapore

An *Original* Publication of POCKET BOOKS

POCKET BOOKS, a division of Simon & Schuster Inc.
1230 Avenue of the Americas, New York, NY 10020

Copyright © 1997 by Tony Pace and Mark Spellen

All rights reserved, including the right to reproduce
this book or portions thereof in any form whatsoever.
For information address Pocket Books, 1230 Avenue
of the Americas, New York, NY 10020

ISBN: 0-671-00952-4

First Pocket Books trade paperback printing August 1997

10 9 8 7 6 5 4 3 2

POCKET and colophon are registered trademarks of
Simon & Schuster Inc.

Cover design by Mike Stromberg

Cover photo credits: top left © Robert Tringali, Jr./Sportschrome, Inc.; top center, Focus on Sports; top right © Robert Tringali, Jr./Sportschrome, Inc.; middle left, Focus on Sports; middle right, Focus on Sports; bottom right, Archive Photos/PNI; bottom center, David L. Johnson/Sportschrome, Inc.

Text design by Stanley S. Drate/Folio Graphics Co. Inc.

Printed in the U.S.A.

DEDICATION

To my family, who made me and kept me a Notre Dame man. Mom, for giving me true Irish blood; Dad, for "making me" a Domer; my brothers, Dan and Tom, for carrying the torch, each in their own way, as ND students and graduates; my sisters, Susan, Macaire, and Cathy, for being rabid Irish football fans.

TONY PACE
February 26, 1997

In fondest memory of my mother, Elizabeth M. Spellen, whose passion for education and life gives me the inspiration to persevere against all odds.

MARK SPELLEN
March 2, 1997

The authors wish to gratefully acknowledge the following people without whose help and support this project would not have been possible:

Tom Ansel
Ross Browner
Tris Coburn
Glen Dansforth
Willie Fry
John Heisler and the UND Sports Information Dept.
John P. Holms
Ellen Hyde
Aina Lakis
Harry and Mara Lakis
Chris and Steve McQuade
Dan Pace
Maureen Pace
Bill Panzica
Dan "Rudy" Ruettiger
Tony Seidl
Adaline Sinigaglia
Bruce Spellen
Suzanne Spellen
Pete Wolverton

CONTENTS

INTRODUCTION

So you think you know about Notre Dame football? You know about Rockne, the Gipper, and the Four Horsemen. But you may not know about some of their exploits. For example, did you know that Rockne was a student journalist, among other things, while he attended Notre Dame? And you may not know that the Four Horsemen played on the only Rockne-coached team to appear in a bowl game. When we started this project we knew some of those facts, but we unearthed many others that were news to us. In many ways that is part of the attraction of Notre Dame football. It is like the proverbial onion: Each time you peel away a layer and discover something new, there is another layer still to be peeled. And with each layer new connections come to light that add to your overall understanding of the subject.

We hope our endeavor adds to your knowledge and enjoyment of Notre Dame football. It is an amazing and continuing story.

Here's one question to get you started:

What did Tony Pace predict for the outcome of the 1978 Cotton Bowl in the preholiday issue of the ND student newspaper, *The Observer?* For the answer see the Final Word.

FIGHTIN' IRISH

Was this player ever a consensus All-American?
(Photo by Brother Charles McBride)

All-Americans

Notre Dame All-Americans. That phrase seems almost magical. And, for a time, it seemed almost redundant. Every year had Irish All-Americans from Rockne to Leahy; the Irish produced All-Americans as if it were their birthright. How could an All-American team be legitimate if there wasn't a Notre Dame player on it? While that notion may seem far-fetched today, consider the continuing quality and national appeal of Notre Dame through college football's formative years. All this is not to say Notre Dame players were picked too easily or given special treatment. Winning teams have quality players . . . and Notre Dame certainly had winning teams.

We are going to highlight some of the major accomplishments of various Irish consensus All-Americans and leave one blank for each of these great athletes for you to fill in.

1913

GUS DORAIS
Quarterback, 5–7, 145, Chippewa Falls, WI

1. Gus was the only four-year starter at quarterback for Notre Dame for 70 years until Blair Kiel in 1980.

2. He, along with Knute Rockne, is credited with making the forward pass popular after the 1913 Army upset with one of the first recorded passes to Rockne.

3. He led Notre Dame to _____ consecutive undefeated seasons.

4. Still holds all-time Notre Dame individual record for most field goals attempted in a single game with seven.

1920

GEORGE GIPP
Halfback, 6–0, 175, Laurium, MI
"The Gipper"

1. Would have become a legend even if he had overcome the streptococcic throat infection that led to his untimely death at the age of _____.

2. His death came just two weeks after he was elected by Walter Camp as Notre Dame's first All-American.

3. His career mark of 2,341 rushing yards lasted more than 50 years until Jerome Heavens broke it in 1978.

4. During Gipp's career, Notre Dame compiled a 27–2–3 record, including a 19–0–1 mark in his last 20 games.

1929–30

FRANK CARIDEO
Quarterback, 5-7, 172, Mt. Vernon, NY

1. 1929 and 1930 quarterback for undefeated Irish national championship teams.

2. A unanimous first-team All-America quarterback in 1929 and '30 who scored the only touchdown in a shutout win over Penn State during 1928 season.

3. In _____ last game vs. USC in 1930 Frank called a play that resulted in his receiving a pass from Marchy Schwartz for a 19-yard TD.

4. He is second on all-time list for total kick returns in a career with 96 and holds career per-game record at 3.4.

1930–31

MARCHY SCHWARTZ
Halfback, 5-11, 167, Bay St. Louis, MS

1. Marchy was a two-time consensus halfback who helped the Irish to the 1930 national title and was a unanimous All-America pick as a senior in 1931.

2. He ranked second behind George Gipp on Notre Dame career rushing list when he finished his career.

3. He still holds record for most _____ in a game with 15 vs. Army in 1931.

4. He rushed for 1,945 career yards on 355 carries for 16 TDs and still stands 10th on the Irish career rushing list.

1946-47

GEORGE CONNOR
Tackle, 6–3, 225, Chicago, IL

1. Won the Outland Trophy in 1946 as outstanding guard or tackle.

2. In 1948 participated in East-West Shrine game.

3. George was a first-round draft pick in 1946 of the NFL team _____.

4. He also played eight years in the NFL, and in 1963 was elected to National Football Foundation Hall of Fame.

1946-47

JOHN LUJACK
Quarterback, 6–0, 180, Connellsville, PA

1. Lujack became the quarterback for Notre Dame as a sophomore in 1943 when Angelo Bertelli joined the Marines.

2. He led Irish to three national titles and established a reputation as one of the great _____ in college football history.

3. He spent three years in the navy, but returned in time to earn consensus All-American honors as a junior and senior on Notre Dame teams in '46 and '47.

4. Was a first-round draft pick by the Chicago Bears, where he played for four years.

1947-48

BILL FISCHER
Tackle, 6–2, 230, Chicago, IL

1. Was captain of Irish team in '48 as a three-year starter in 1946–48 on teams that never lost a game and claimed national titles in '46 and '47.

2. He led all Irish linemen in 1947 with 300 minutes of play.

3. First-round pick in 1949 NFL draft by _____.

4. He returned to Notre Dame in 1954 to coach under Terry Brennan.

1948-49

EMIL "RED" SITKO
Fullback, 5–8, 175, Ft. Wayne, IN

1. A two-time consensus All-American selection at fullback who was a unanimous pick while helping Irish to the 1949 national title.

2. "Red" never played in a _____ while at Notre Dame.

3. In 1948 he led the team with 742 yards on 129 carries and nine TDs, caught seven passes for 70 yards, and returned one kickoff 76 yards.

4. "Red" played three seasons in the NFL with San Francisco and the Chicago Cardinals.

1959

MONTY STICKLES
End, 6–4, 215, Poughkeepsie, NY

1. This three-year starter at end, played from 1957 to 1959, and was a two-time first-team All-American.

2. He had 11 catches for 183 yards and three touchdowns in '57 and led the team in scoring with 11 PATs, one field goal, and three TDs for 32 points.

3. He led the team in _____ in 1958 and scored 60 points while making 31 tackles.

4. Monty was a first-round NFL draft choice in 1960 by San Francisco.

1964

JACK SNOW
Split End, 6–2, 210, Long Beach, CA

1. He finished fifth in Heisman Trophy voting as a senior in 1964 behind teammate John Huarte.

2. In the 1964 season opener against Wisconsin he caught nine passes for 217 yards and two touchdowns.

3. Those 217 receiving yards set Irish single-game best and also set record for receiving TDs that was not broken until 1994.

4. First-round NFL draft pick of Los Angeles Rams in 1965 and played through 19 _____.

1966

ALAN PAGE

Defensive End, 6–5, 230, Canton, OH

1. A three-year starter as defensive right end from 1964–66 who had 63 tackles in '66 while helping Irish to a national title.

2. He made 134 career tackles, recovered four fumbles, broke up two passes, and scored one touchdown.

3. In 1967 Alan was a first-round choice of Minnesota in 1967 NFL draft as 15th overall selection.

4. He played in four Super Bowls with the Vikings and was elected to _____ in 1993.

1966

TOM REGNER

Offensive Guard, 6–1, 250, Kenosha, WI

1. A two-year regular at left offensive guard in 1965 and 1966 after starting at right defensive tackle as a sophomore in 1964.

2. He had 68 tackles in 1964, then moved to offensive guard and was member of 1966 national championship team.

3. Also a 1966 CoSIDA Academic All-American and a member of 1967 College All-Star team.

4. He was picked by _____ in the first round of 1967 NFL draft as 23rd overall selection.

1969

MIKE McCOY

Defensive Tackle, 6–5, 270, Erie, PA

1. Unanimous first-team All-American as senior in 1969.

2. Named Lineman of the Week by _____ after defeat of Northwestern in 1969.

3. He accumulated a total of 203 career tackles, two for losses, and intercepted two passes.

4. Chosen by Green Bay in first round of 1970 NFL draft as second overall player selected.

1970

TOM GATEWOOD

Split End, 6–2, 203, Baltimore, MD

1. The 1971 Irish cocaptain who led the Irish in receiving in 1969 with 47 for 743 yards, 1970 with 77 for 1,123, and 1971 with 33 for 417.

2. Currently holds records for most passes caught in a season (77 for 1,123 yards).

3. Also record holder for most passes caught in a career with 157 for 2,283 yards; most catches per game in a season with 7.7; most touchdowns by reception in a game (3) and in a career with 19.

4. Played in 1972 _____ Bowl.

1971

WALT PATULSKI

Defensive End, 6–6, 235, Liverpool, NY

1. Walt was a unanimous All-American and three-year starter at left defensive end as well as '71 Irish cocaptain.

2. He started every game in his collegiate career, racking up 186 tackles, 40 for minus 241 yards; broke up 10 passes; recovered five fumbles; and returned one blocked punt 12 yards.

3. He played in the _____ and _____ All-Star games in 1972.

4. Was first-round draft pick in 1972 by Buffalo as first overall selection.

1974

GERRY DiNARDO

Guard, 6–1, 242, Howard Beach, NY

1. He was a member of 1973 Irish national championship team.

2. He helped Notre Dame to 3,502 rushing yards, an all-time Irish record.

3. Gerry is currently serving as head football coach at _____ after previously serving as head coach at _____.

4. He coached against Notre Dame in the 1991 _____ Bowl.

1975

STEVE NIEHAUS
Defensive Tackle, 6–5, 270, Cincinnati, OH

1. Steve "The House" Niehaus finished 12th in Heisman Trophy voting and was All-American by unanimous selection as senior in 1975.

2. He had 95 tackles, 13 for minus 82 yards; broke up two passes; and recovered one fumble in '74.

3. His career totals at Notre Dame included 290 tackles, 25 for minus 128 yards.

4. He was a first-round choice of _____ in 1976 NFL draft as second overall selection.

1976–77

KEN MacAFEE
Tight End, 6–5, 251, Brockton, MA

1. He was a three-time first-team All-American in 1975–77 and a unanimous pick in '77 as a senior.

2. During the 1977 national championship season he caught 54 passes for 797 yards and 6 touchdowns.

3. He caught 128 career passes for 1,759 yards and 15 TDs, ranking third on Notre Dame career receiving chart.

4. Currently is a _____.

1976-77

ROSS BROWNER
Defensive End, 6-3, 240, Warren, OH

1. Four-year Irish starter who played on 1973 and 1977 national championship teams.

2. Unanimous first team All-America end in both _____ and _____.

3. Holds Notre Dame record for tackles for lost yardage in a career with 77.

4. Was first-round NFL draft pick of Cincinnati Bengals and played through 1987 season.

1977

LUTHER BRADLEY
Strong Safety, 6-2, 200, Muncie, IN

1. Played on 1973 and 1977 Irish national championship teams.

2. Had 153 career tackles, broke up 27 passes, recovered two fumbles, and blocked two kicks.

3. Holds all-time Notre Dame individual record for most _____ in a career with 17 for 218 yards.

4. 1978 Japan Bowl participant and was drafted in 1978 in the first round by Detroit and played through 1981.

1979

VAGAS FERGUSON
Halfback, 6–1, 194, Richmond, IN

1. Finished his career as Notre Dame's all-time leading ground gainer with 3,472 rushing yards and 32 touchdowns.

2. He was the first Irish rusher to gain more than 1,000 yards in consecutive seasons with 1,437 in 1979 following 1,192 in '78.

3. He was a member of 1977 national championship team and was named outstanding offensive player of 1978 Cotton Bowl with 100 rushing yards and three TDs.

4. Holds all-time record for rushing yards in a game with 255 vs. _____ in 1978.

1980–81

BOB CRABLE
Linebacker, 6–3, 225, Cincinnati, OH

1. Was a near unanimous All-America pick in both 1980 and '81 with 521 career tackles, still a Notre Dame record.

2. Crable holds the records for most tackles in a season (187 in 1979) and in a game (26 vs. Clemson in 1979).

3. He _____ during the 1979 Cotton Bowl, which led to Irish TD and comeback victory.

4. In 1979 he won the Michigan game with a last-second field goal block.

1987

TIM BROWN

Flanker, 6–0, 195, Dallas, TX

1. Brown utilized his ability as a pass receiver, rusher, and punt and kickoff returner to rank third nationally in all-purpose yardage as a junior (176.5 per game) and sixth as a senior (167.9).

2. He finished his career at Notre Dame as the all-time leader in pass reception yards (2,493).

3. He also returned _____ kicks for touchdowns.

4. Brown was a first-round pick of the Los Angeles Raiders in the 1988 NFL draft.

1989–90

TODD LYGHT

Cornerback, 6–1, 184, Flint, MI

1. Two-time consensus All-American in 1989 and 1990; unanimous pick as junior in '89.

2. Todd had more playing time in 1987 than any other freshman, making 29 tackles, causing one fumble, breaking up two passes, and making one interception.

3. He led the team in tackles in '89 Fiesta Bowl win over West Virginia for the national championship.

4. He was ranked _____ in final NCAA standings in '89 for interceptions.

1992-93

AARON TAYLOR
Offensive Tackle, 6–4, 280, Concord, CA

1. A unanimous first-team All-America selection in 1992 as senior offensive tackle.

2. He was winner of the 1992 _____ Award.

3. He was also captain of the team his senior season, starting 30 games straight to end his career.

4. Drafted by Green Bay Packers in the first round of 1994 NFL selections.

1993

JEFF BURRIS
Free Safety, 6–0, 204, Rock Hill, SC

1. 1993 tri-captain of Irish squad that went 11–1 and who led 1992 team in _____ and _____ played.

2. He was consistently ranked nationally in 1991 as punt returner with final 12.6-yard average.

3. Played more minutes in 1993 than any other Irish defensive player, with career totals: 89 tackles, 14 passes broken up; 10 interceptions for 67 yards; 29 carries for 136 yards and 10 TDs.

4. Irish MVP in 1993 win over top-rated Florida State; was a first-round selection in 1994 by Buffalo Bills.

All-American
ANSWERS

1913	Dorais—3
1920	Gipp—25
1929–30	Carideo—Knute Rockne's
1930–31	Schwartz—punts
1946–47	Connor—NY Giants
1946–47	Lujack—T-formation signal callers
1947–48	Fischer—Chicago Cardinals
1948–49	Sitko—losing game
1959	Stickles—minutes played
1964	Snow—75
1966	Page—NFL Hall of Fame
1966	Regner—Houston
1969	McCoy—*Sports Illustrated*
1970	Gatewood—Hula
1971	Patulski—College All-Star and Hula
1974	DiNardo—LSU, Vanderbilt
1975	Niehaus—Seattle
1976–77	Browner—1976, 1977
1976–77	MacAfee—oral surgeon
1977	Bradley—interceptions
1979	Ferguson—Georgia Tech
1980–81	Crable—recovered a Houston fumble
1987	Brown—6
1989–90	Lyght—8th
1992–93	Taylor—Lombardi
1993	Burris—interceptions and minutes

Bowl Games

The Irish played only one bowl game in the Rockne era (do you know which one?) and then decided not to participate in bowl games again until 1970. The main reason for this 45-year moratorium was the game's interference with the school's academic schedule. But times change. Players saw them as a reward, the

exposure certainly didn't hurt, and the financial payoffs were growing dramatically because of television's increasing demand for sports programming.

By the way, the only Rockne bowl game? The 1925 Rose Bowl against Stanford. To this day, it is Notre Dame's only appearance in "the granddaddy of them all."

Here are the Notre Dame seniors who played in the January 1, 1978 Cotton Bowl victory against Texas.
(Photo courtesy of University of Notre Dame Sports Information Dept.)

Bowl Bits
(Multiple Choice)

1. Name the only member of the Four Horsemen to score a touchdown in the 1925 Rose Bowl.

   A. Henry Stuhldreher
   B. Elmer Layden
   C. Jim Crowley
   D. Don Miller

2. How did Layden score his three touchdowns in that game?

   A. Three runs
   B. Two runs and one punt return
   C. One run and two interception returns
   D. One run, one punt return, one interception

3. In their first bowl game after the 45-year moratorium, Notre Dame did the following.

   A. Beat Texas 21–17 in the Cotton Bowl
   B. Beat Texas 24–11 in the Cotton Bowl
   C. Lost to Texas 21–17 in the Orange Bowl
   D. Lost to Texas 21–17 in the Orange Bowl

4. This Heisman Trophy winner found the end zone four times as his team routed the Irish in the 1973 Orange Bowl.

   A. Jeff Kinney
   B. Johnny Rodgers
   C. Steve Owen
   D. Greg Pruitt

5. This 1976 bowl game scored not one play from then sophomore Joe Montana.

   A. Orange Bowl versus Alabama
   B. Gator Bowl versus Penn State
   C. Cotton Bowl versus Texas
   D. Cotton Bowl versus Houston

6. After splitting time with Montana in 1975, this Irish quarterback led them to a 20–9 win versus Penn State in the 1976 Gator Bowl.

   A. Gary Forystek
   B. Rusty Lisch
   C. Cliff Brown
   D. Rick Slager

7. This was Notre Dame's farewell win for Ara Parseghian.

   A. Orange Bowl victory versus Nebraska
   B. Orange Bowl victory versus Alabama
   C. Sugar Bowl victory versus Alabama
   D. Cotton Bowl victory versus Texas

8. This was Gerry Faust's only bowl win as Notre Dame's head coach.

   A. 1983 Liberty Bowl
   B. 1984 Aloha Bowl
   C. 1980 Sugar Bowl
   D. 1985 Orange Bowl

9. In the 1979 Cotton Bowl win versus Houston, Notre Dame trailed the Cougars 34–12 with 7:35 left in the game when this play happened.

    A. Montana touchdown pass to Kris Haines
    B. Montana touchdown pass to Pete Holohan
    C. Jerome Heavens touchdown run
    D. Steve Cichy return of a blocked punt for 33 yards

10. Who among the following Notre Dame Heisman Trophy winners is the only one to play a bowl game?

    A. John Huarte
    B. Paul Hornung
    C. Elmer Layden
    D. Tim Brown

11. Which Notre Dame coach in the modern era has the best winning percentage in bowl games?

    A. Ara Parseghian
    B. Lou Holtz
    C. Dan Devine
    D. Gerry Faust

12. Which Heisman Trophy winner gained the most yards against Notre Dame in a bowl game?

    A. Johnny Rodgers
    B. Earl Campbell
    C. Herschel Walker
    D. Steve Wooster

Bowl Matchup Quiz
(one name used more than once)

Match the correct answer from the right-hand column with the question in the left-hand column.

WHAT?	WHO?
1. This freshman took a kickoff back 93 yards for a touchdown in the 1974 Sugar Bowl.	**A.** Derrick Mayes
2. He caught the winning score from Joe Montana in the classic 1979 Cotton Bowl comeback versus Houston.	**B.** Joe Montana
3. His much debated clipping penalty negated Rocket Ismail's 91-yard touchdown run that would have beaten eventual National Champion Colorado in the '91 Orange Bowl.	**C.** Tony Rice
4. He was featured on the cover of *Sports Illustrated* after the 1978 Cotton Bowl win versus Texas.	**D.** Joe Unis
5. This Irish running back scored three touchdowns in 1978 Cotton Bowl win versus Texas (38–10).	**E.** Kris Haines
6. This Irish quarterback has thrown the most interceptions in bowl games.*	**F.** Ron Powlus

WHAT?	WHO?
7. This Irish running back has scored the most points in a bowl game.	**G.** Tony Rice
8. This Notre Dame quarterback shares the record for most touchdown passes in a bowl game with Ron Powlus.	**H.** Al Hunter
9. This running back was the only Notre Dame participant in the 1995 East-West Shrine Classic.	**I.** Vagas Ferguson
10. He won the Heisman Trophy but they stole his towel in the 1988 Cotton Bowl.	**J.** Jerome Heavens
11. He set a record for most yardage per completion in the 1989 Fiesta Bowl.	**K.** Greg Davis
12. He has the record for most kicking points in Notre Dame bowl history.	**L.** Tom Krug
13. This Notre Dame running back holds the record for career rushing attempts in bowl games.	**M.** Jerome Bettis
14. This Notre Dame receiver scored two touchdowns in both the 1995 Fiesta Bowl and 1996 Orange Bowl.	**N.** Tony Rice

WHAT?	WHO?
15. This Notre Dame player ran for one two-point conversion and passed for another in the 1979 Cotton Bowl victory versus Houston.	**O.** Terry Eurick
16. This Notre Dame kicker scored the 35th and winning point to beat Houston 35–34 in the 1979 Cotton Bowl.	**P.** Dave Reeve
17. This tight end, who would later play for the NY Mets organization, caught a touchdown pass in the 1989 Fiesta Bowl victory over West Virginia.	**Q.** Tim Brown
18. Vagas Ferguson had three touchdowns, but this Irish back gained more yards in the 1979 Cotton Bowl.	**R.** Allen Pinkett
19. He was 0 for 3 passing with one interception in the 1988 Cotton Bowl.	**S.** Frank Jacobs
20. He holds the Irish record for the most completions in a bowl game.	**T.** Lee Becton

True or False

1. _____ Jerome Bettis scored at least one touchdown in all three bowl games he appeared in.

2. _____ Joe Montana ran for more touchdowns than he threw in the 1979 Cotton Bowl.

3. _____ The 1979 Cotton Bowl had the lowest attendance of any bowl game Notre Dame has played in.

4. _____ Mark Bavaro never played in a bowl game for Notre Dame.

5. _____ Doug Flutie didn't score against Notre Dame in the 1984 Liberty Bowl.

6. _____ Al Hunter was the first Notre Dame back to go over 100 yards rushing in a bowl game with 102 yards versus Penn State in the Gator Bowl.

7. _____ Joe Theismann had the most carries against Texas, 18–22, in the 1971 Cotton Bowl win.

8. _____ Georgia had only one complete pass in their 1981 Sugar Bowl win versus Notre Dame.

9. _____ Rocket Ismail never scored a touchdown in a bowl game.

10. _____ Notre Dame has appeared in the Orange Bowl more often than any other bowl game.

Bowl Bits
ANSWERS

1. **B:** Elmer Layden scored not once, not twice, but three times in the Irish 27–10 win over the Stanford Indians.

2. **C:** Long before Dion Sanders, Layden was showing you could score from both sides of the ball with interception returns of 70 and 78 yards to go with a three-yard rushing touchdown.

3. **D:** Texas used two fourth-quarter touchdowns to outlast the Irish in the 1970 Cotton Bowl. Notre Dame would exact its revenge on Texas the following year with a 24–11 win.

4. **B:** Rodgers led a 40–6 blowout by Nebraska with three rushing touchdowns and one pass reception for a score.

5. **B:** Montana sustained a shoulder injury that sidelined him for the 1976 season, so he didn't participate in the Gator Bowl game.

6. **D:** Slager played error-free football to lead the Irish to the victory. He was aided by Al Hunter's 102 yards rushing and two touchdowns.

7. **B:** For the second straight year, Parseghian beat Bear Bryant as the Irish prevailed 13–11.

8. **A:** Faust's Irish topped the Boston College Eagles 19–18 for his only bowl win.

9. **D:** Tony Belden blocked it and fellow freshman Cichy returned it 33 yards to start the miraculous comeback.

10. **D:** Only Brown has done it. Layden didn't win the Heisman because there wasn't one in his day.

11. **C:** Dan Devine was 3–1 in bowl games. Parseghian 3–2, Gerry Faust 1–1, and Lou Holtz is 5–4 entering the 1996 bowl season.

12. **C:** Worster actually outgained Walker, 155 to 150, but he didn't win the Heisman Trophy.

Bowl Matchup
ANSWERS

1. **H,** Al Hunter

2. **E,** Kris Haines

3. **K,** Greg Davis

4. **O,** Terry Eurick

5. **I,** Vagas Ferguson

6. **B,** Joe Montana *Joe threw 5 interceptions in the 1978 and 1979 Cotton Bowls.

7. **M,** Jerome Bettis

8. **L,** Tom Krug

9. **T,** Lee Becton

10. **Q,** Tim Brown

11. **G, N, C,** Tony Rice

12. **P,** Dave Reeve

13. **R,** Allen Pinkett

14. **A,** Derrick Mayes

15. **B,** Joe Montana

16. **D,** Joe Unis

17. **S,** Frank Jacobs

18. **J,** Jerome Heavens

19. **C, G, N,** Tony Rice

20. **F,** Ron Powlus

True or False
ANSWERS

1. **False.** Although he ran well in the '91 Orange Bowl, Bettis didn't score in that game.

2. **True.** Montana ran for two scores in the game and only threw for the winning score.

3. **True.** Announced attendance at the Ice Bowl game was 32,500, and far fewer were around to see the Irish rally for a memorable victory. The previous year over 76,000 witnessed Notre Dame's 38–10 Cotton Bowl triumph against Texas.

4. **False.** Bavaro played in both the 1983 Liberty Bowl and 1984 Aloha Bowl.

5. **True.** But the recipients of three of his passes did. Brian Brennan, Gerard Phelan, and Scott Gieselman did.

6. **True.** Notre Dame had some good performances, notably by Wayne Bullock in the 1973 Sugar Bowl and 1975 Orange Bowl, but Hunter was the first over the century mark.

7. **True.** Remarkable but true. Theismann scored twice on runs of 3 and 15 yards. Two other backs had 13 carries each, but Theismann topped them.

8. **Unfortunately True.** Buck Belue was 1 for 12 for seven yards and Herschel Walker was 0 for 1 on an option pass, yet the Bulldogs still prevailed and won the national title.

9. **False.** He caught a touchdown pass from Tony Rice in the 1989 Fiesta Bowl and ran for a 35-yard score in the 1990 Orange Bowl.

10. **False.** The Orange Bowl runs a close second to the Cotton Bowl with five and seven appearances respectively.

Dan Devine won a national championship in 1977, yet is still not considered in the upper echelon of Notre Dame coaches.
(Photo courtesy of University of Notre Dame Sports Information Dept.)

Championships

Those championship seasons. At Notre Dame that means national championship, since the university doesn't belong to a conference. Plays, players, and games from championship seasons are immortalized . . . creating memories and moments that fans reminisce about at least until the next championship. Here are some brain teasers from Notre Dame's storied championship history.

Championship Choices

1. Which of the following teams was not rated higher than Notre Dame prior to the 1978 Cotton Bowl game?

   A. Oklahoma
   B. Texas
   C. Alabama
   D. Arkansas

2. The 1973 Sugar Bowl win versus Alabama that sealed that year's national championship featured a memorable pass from Tom Clements to this Irish tight end to get Notre Dame out of precarious field position.

   A. Ken MacAfee
   B. Mike Creaney
   C. Dave Casper
   D. Robin Weber

3. Who stepped in at quarterback for Notre Dame when Terry Hanratty was injured in the famous 10–10 tie with Michigan State during the 1966 national championship season?

   A. Bill Etter
   B. Tom Schoen
   C. Coley O'Brien
   D. Joe Theismann

4. Which of the following players was not a captain of a national championship team?

   A. Leon Hart
   B. Jim Lynch
   C. Bob Golic
   D. Willie Fry

5. Which Notre Dame player neither played nor coached on a national championship team?

   A. Elmer Layden
   B. Terry Brennan
   C. Terry Hanratty
   D. Joe Theismann

6. Which member of the Four Horsemen led Notre Dame in scoring during their '24 championship year?

   A. Don Miller
   B. Elmer Layden
   C. Harry Stuhldreher
   D. Jim Crowley

7. Which player led the '88 championship team in receiving?

   A. Derek Brown
   B. Tim Brown
   C. Rocket Ismail
   D. Ricky Watters

8. Which player was the rushing leader of the '77 championship team?

   A. Vagas Ferguson
   B. Al Hunter
   C. Jerome Heavens
   D. Wayne Bullock

9. Which player was the rushing leader of the 1988 national championship team?

   A. Mark Green
   B. Anthony Johnson
   C. Tony Brooks
   D. Tony Rice

10. Which team interrupted Notre Dame's championship streak from '46–'49 by winning the title in 1948?

A. Michigan
B. Oklahoma
C. Army
D. Ohio State

Championship Matches

Match each ND championship team with its pivotal win or tie.

1. 1977 team		**A.** USC 38–7
2. 1988 team		**B.** Michigan State 10–10
3. 1943 team		**C.** Miami 31–30
4. 1966 team		**D.** Army 0–0
5. 1973 team		**E.** Army 13–0
6. 1924 team		**F.** Army 7–6
7. 1946 team		**G.** Alabama 24–23
8. 1947 team		**H.** Michigan 35–12
9. 1930 team		**I.** USC 49–19

T he culmination of any great season is not just winning games but winning championships. This represents an elite position in the sports world. As a team we remained committed and focused on winning championships, from the start of each season to the very end. Of course history has shown we were pretty good at it!

Willie Fry, All-American Defensive End
1973 and 1977 ND Championship Teams

Championship True or False

1. _____ Frank Leahy won more national titles at Notre Dame than Knute Rockne.

2. _____ Prior to 1977 Notre Dame never won a national title with a loss on their record.

3. _____ Dan Devine never won a national championship at Notre Dame.

4. _____ Lou Holtz was coach for one national title while at Notre Dame, but he can claim an assist on another.

5. _____ Even though they were ranked #1 at the time, Notre Dame was a 10-point underdog against USC in the last regular-season game of 1988.

6. _____ The longest championship draught in Notre Dame history was from the Leahy '49 squad to the Parseghian '66 team.

7. _____ George Gipp was a member of the 1924 national championship team.

8. _____ Notre Dame has never had a Heisman Trophy winner in a national championship season.

Championship Choice
ANSWERS

1. **D:** Arkansas was rated behind the Irish at the end of the 1977 regular season.

2. **D:** Clements to Weber for 35 yards moved Notre Dame to much better field position and helped ensure a 24–23 victory.

3. **C:** O'Brien, who had been diagnosed with diabetes only a few weeks earlier, rallied the Irish from a 10–0 deficit.

4. **C:** Golic captained the 1978 squad, the year following the championship.

5. **D:** Theismann was on the freshman team in 1966, but freshmen were not eligible to play with the varsity at that time.

6. **D:** Crowley scored nine touchdowns, but he also had the advantage of being the kicker, which meant another 17 points for his total.

7. **D:** Watters did with 15 catches, the lowest total since 1965.

8. **C:** For the second time in three years Heavens led all rushers, this time falling just short of 1,000 yards with a final total of 994.

9. **D:** Yes, quarterback Tony Rice led the '88 champs in rushing with 700 yards. He did again in '89 as well with 884 yards.

10. **A:** The Wolverines won the title in '48; they haven't done so since then.

Matchups
ANSWERS

1. **I,** USC	49–19	**5.** **G,** Alabama	24–23
2. **C,** Miami	31–30	**6.** **E,** Army	13–0
3. **H,** Michigan	35–12	**7.** **D,** Army	0–0
4. **B,** Michigan State	10–10	**8.** **A,** USC	38–7
		9. **F,** Army	7–6

Championship True or False
ANSWERS

1. **True.** Leahy is credited with four national titles to Rockne's three.

2. **False.** In 1943 they lost their season-ending game to Great Lakes yet were still voted #1. Notre Dame's team finished 9–1 but had been depleted due to World War II call-ups.

3. **False.** Devine's 1977 squad jumped from 5th to 1st in the final poll with a 38–10 rout of prebowl #1 Texas.

4. **True.** His Arkansas Razorbacks upset #2 Oklahoma in the Orange Bowl to help the 1977 Irish vault to the top spot.

5. **True.** The Irish, at that point, did not have a good history in the Los Angeles Coliseum.

6. **False.** Notre Dame was playing football for 31 years before it won its first national title with Knute Rockne's '24 team.

7. **False.** Gipp played for the Irish in 1917–20. He passed away on December 14, 1920, from a throat infection.

8. **False.** Three times the Irish have won titles with a player winning the Heisman Award: '43 Bertelli, '47 Lujack, and '49 Hart.

Draft Choices

The linkage between Notre Dame and the National Football League was established early on. Elmer Layden, one of the famed Four Horsemen, was NFL commissioner in the 1930s. "Hunk" Anderson, another Notre Dame coach, was up in Green Bay working with the Packers. Later on, Notre Dame men like Joe Kuharich moved back and forth between their alma mater and NFL jobs. In recent years that linkage has been strongest in terms of players. Since the advent of the draft in 1936, 410 Notre Dame players have been chosen by professional teams.

Select Choices

1. Which NFL team selected John Huarte but lost him to the NY Jets in an AFL-NFL bidding war?

   A. New York Giants
   B. Kansas City Chiefs
   C. Chicago Bears
   D. Philadelphia Eagles

Terry Hanratty was drafted by the Pittsburgh Steelers.
(Photo courtesy of University of Notre Dame Sports Information Dept.)

2. Who was the quarterback Bill Walsh wanted in 1979 when he ended up with Joe Montana in the third round?

   A. Jack Thompson
   B. Steve Fuller
   C. Phil Simms
   D. Steve Deberg

3. Bob Golic had a great NFL career with the Browns and the Raiders but neither of those teams drafted him. Who did?

   A. New York Jets
   B. Chicago Bears
   C. Atlanta Falcons
   D. New England Patriots

4. Besides Golic, one other Notre Dame player was selected before Montana in 1979. Who was he?

   A. Jerome Heavens
   B. Ken MacAfee
   C. Luther Bradley
   D. Dave Huffman

5. The last Notre Dame player to be the overall first selection in the draft is:

   A. Rick Mirer
   B. Walt Patulski
   C. Rocket Ismail
   D. Tim Brown

6. Which of these Irish quarterbacks was not drafted in the first round?

   A. Paul Hornung
   B. George Izo
   C. Joe Theismann
   D. Ralph Guglielmi

7. Which of these Irish running backs did not get selected in the first round?

   A. Vagas Ferguson
   B. Allen Pinkett
   C. Greg Bell
   D. Jerome Bettis

8. In what round did the Steelers select Rocky Bleier in the 1968 NFL draft?

   A. Fifth
   B. Tenth
   C. Twelfth
   D. Sixteenth

9. Who was the Notre Dame player selected prior to future Hall of Famer Alan Page in 1967?

   A. Kevin Hardy
   B. Paul Seiler
   C. Tom Regner
   D. George Kunz

10. Which Brooks brother was selected higher when he entered the NFL?

   A. Tony
   B. Reggie

11. Which Irish line stalwart went higher in the 1994 draft?

   A. Aaron Taylor
   B. Bryant Young

12. Who was the last Notre Dame wide receiver to be drafted in the first round?

   A. Derrick Mayes
   B. Rocket Ismail
   C. Jim Seymour
   D. Tim Brown

True or False

1. _____ The most Notre Dame players drafted in one season is ten in 1994.

2. _____ Lou Holtz has had one of his players selected in the first or second round every year at Notre Dame through 1996.

3. _____ Wide receiver Jim Seymour was selected before his pitcher, quarterback Terry Hanratty, in 1969.

4. _____ Steve Beuerlein lasted until the fourth round despite a stellar senior season as Irish quarterback.

5. _____ Ross Browner was the only member of his clan to be selected in the first round of the NFL draft.

6. _____ The fewest Irish players selected in any draft since 1960 is two in 1976 after Dan Devine's first year.

7. _____ John Carney, the longtime Charger kicker, was never drafted.

8. _____ Dave Huffman was the only one of his brothers who was ever drafted.

9. _____ Irish quarterback Tom Clements was never drafted.

10. _____ Before Ara Parseghian, no Notre Dame players were selected in the first round in the early sixties.

Player Matchups

Match these Irish players with the NFL teams who originally drafted them.

WHO?	WHERE?
1. Steve Beuerlein	**A.** NY Giants
2. Andy Heck	**B.** Indianapolis Colts
3. Bob Golic	**C.** Miami Dolphins
4. Frank Stams	**D.** LA Rams
5. Willie Fry	**E.** Philadelphia Eagles
6. Bob Kuechenberg	**F.** Pittsburgh Steelers
7. Jerome Bettis	**G.** LA Rams
8. Joe Theismann	**H.** New England Patriots
9. Anthony Johnson	**I.** Seattle Seahawks
10. Derek Brown	**J.** LA Raiders

Select Choice
ANSWERS

1. **D:** Philly had acquired Norm Snead from Washington to be their quarterback and didn't bid aggressively against the Jets.

2. **C:** Walsh loved Simms, but the Giants shocked everyone when they took Simms with the seventh pick overall.

3. **D:** The Patriots let Golic play linebacker, his preferred position, before waiving him. The Browns converted him to nose guard, where he enjoyed his professional success.

4. **D:** The Vikings tabbed Huffman in round two of the 1979 draft.

5. **B:** Ismail would have gone #1 if he hadn't jumped to the Canadian Football League prior to the draft.

6. **C:** Theismann was another "NFL-jumper," going to the CFL before he played in the NFL, and that affected his selection position.

7. **B:** Notre Dame's all-time leading rusher went in the third round to the Houston Oilers.

8. **D:** Rocky was selected in a round they don't even have anymore. Yet he has Super Bowl rings to show for his career.

9. **B:** Guard Seiler went 12th overall to, who else, the Jets. The Vikings took Page later and had a player for the ages.

10. **B:** Reggie went with the 45th pick in 1993 to Washington, while Tony lasted until the 92nd pick by the Eagles, a year earlier.

11. **B:** Young went on the seventh overall to San Francisco, while Taylor went nine picks later to Green Bay in 1994.

12. **D:** Brown went 6th overall in 1988.

True or False
ANSWERS

1. **False.** Several earlier drafts had more picks, 11 in 1969 and 13 in 1950.

2. **True.**

3. **True.** But Hanratty had the longer career.

4. **True.**

5. **False.** Brothers Joey and Keith also went in round one despite having played for USC.

6. **True.** Steve Niehaus went second overall to Seattle and cocaptain Ed Bauer went on the seventh round to New Orleans.

7. **True.** But hard to believe.

8. **False.** Tim was drafted in the ninth round by Green Bay.

9. **True.** But equally hard to believe.

10. **False.** George Izo and Monty Stickles were first-round picks in 1960.

Player Matchups

1. **J**, LA Raiders
2. **I**, Seattle Seahawks
3. **H**, New England Patriots
4. **D**, **G**, LA Rams
5. **F**, Pittsburgh Steelers

6. **E**, Philadelphia Eagles
7. **D**, **G**, LA Rams
8. **C**, Miami Dolphins
9. **B**, Indianapolis Colts
10. **A**, NY Giants

Few ND receivers were more exciting than "the Rocket."
(Photo by Greg Kohs)

Ends of the Offensive Nature (Split Ends and Wide Receivers)

Under Lou Holtz, Notre Dame gained the reputation of being an option school, even though the most decorated receiver in Irish history played for Holtz. But many great receivers have donned an Irish uniform over the years. This chapter will test your knowledge of who they are.

Choose the Catchers

1. At the top of the career receivers list for ND, who has the highest average yards per catch?

   A. Tom Gatewood
   B. Jack Snow
   C. Tim Brown
   D. Derrick Mayes

2. He's the only tight end in the top five career receivers for ND.

    A. Irv Smith
    B. Derek Brown
    C. Ken MacAfee
    D. Mark Bavaro

3. This receiver caught the longest pass in Notre Dame history.

    A. Tim Brown
    B. Joe Howard
    C. Rocket Ismail
    D. Tony Smith

4. This former quarterback who later became a defensive back scored a crucial touchdown on an 80-yard pass reception versus North Carolina in 1975.

    A. Joe Restic
    B. Jim Browner
    C. Reggie Barnett
    D. Ted Burgmeier

5. Which receiver scored touchdowns the first three times he touched the ball?

    A. Tim Brown
    B. Kris Haines
    C. Rocket Ismail
    D. Derrick Mayes

6. This end helped popularize the forward pass.

  A. Don Miller
  B. Jim Mutscheller
  C. Knute Rockne
  D. Bernie Kirk

7. Which Notre Dame receiver has the longest kickoff return on a modern field?

  A. Tim Brown
  B. Rocket Ismail
  C. Clint Johnson

8. Who is the second leading career receiver at TE behind Ken MacAfee with 120 receptions?

  A. Derek Brown
  B. Dean Masztak
  C. Irv Smith
  D. Tony Hunter

9. What Notre Dame player holds the national record for yards per catch in one game?

  A. Tim Brown
  B. Rocket Ismail
  C. Derrick Mayes
  D. Jim Morse

10. Who held the Notre Dame career record for yards per catch until it was broken by the Rocket?

  A. Tim Brown
  B. Jim Morse
  C. Joe Howard
  D. Kris Haines

11. He is the only Notre Dame receiver to have over 60 receptions in one season.

   A. Jack Snow
   B. Tom Gatewood
   C. Tim Brown
   D. Derrick Mayes

12. This tight end caught a highlight film touchdown from Rick Mirer versus Indiana in 1991 when he dragged multiple tacklers into the end zone.

   A. Derek Brown
   B. Leon Wallace
   C. Oscar McBride
   D. Irv Smith

Match by the Numbers

Which receiver wore which number. (Numbers can be used more than once.)

1. Tom Gatewood	A. 86
2. Tim Brown	B. 44
3. Derrick Mayes	C. 25
4. Ken MacAfee	D. 86
5. Kris Haines	E. 86
6. Jack Snow	F. 91
7. Rocket Ismail	G. 81

8.	Jim Seymour	**H.**	no number
9.	Pete Demmerle	**I.**	81
10.	Dave Casper	**J.**	85
11.	Mike Creaney	**K.**	85
12.	Dean Masztak	**L.**	1
13.	Tony Hunter	**M.**	82
14.	Knute Rockne	**N.**	85
15.	Derek Brown	**O.**	85

Choose the Catcher
ANSWERS

1. **D:** Mayes had 19.4 yards per catch, while Brown had 18.2.

2. **C:** MacAfee had 128 career receptions, including 54 in his senior season of 1977.

3. **B:** Howard caught a Blair Kiel pass and ran 96 yards for a touchdown against Georgia Tech in 1981.

4. **D:** Ted Burgmeier helped Joe Montana start his reputation for comebacks in this game.

5. **D:** This is one record that won't be broken by the 10th printing of this book.

6. **C:** Rockne caught passes before the Irish even started keeping statistics for receptions.

7. **C:** Clint Johnson took a kickoff back 100 yards versus Stanford in 1993. Alfred Bergman took one back 105

yards versus Loyola, Chicago, in 1911, but that was on a 110-yard field and wasn't even a touchdown despite the length.

8. **D:** Hunter had eight fewer catches but his 1,897 yards outgained MacAfee.

9. **D:** Morse had an amazing 41.6-yards-per-catch average versus USC in 1955 when he caught 5 passes for 208 yards.

10. **D:** The pride of Grace Hall's football contingent had a 21.5-yards-per-catch average from 1975–79.

11. **B:** Gatewood had 77 receptions in 1970 as Joe Theismann chased the Heisman.

12. **D:** Smith made the highlight play of the year in college football.

Player Match
ANSWERS

1. **B,** Tom Gatewood — 44

2. **G,I,** Tim Brown — 81

3. **L,** Derrick Mayes — 1

4. **I,** Ken MacAfee — 81

5. **M,** Kris Haines — 82

6. **N,J,O,C,** Jack Snow — 85

7. **C,** Rocket Ismail — 25

8. **N,J,O,C,** Jim Seymour — 85

9. **N,J,O,C,** Pete Demmerle — 85

10. **A,D,E,** Dave Casper — 86

11. **F,** Mike Creaney — 91

12. **A,D,E,** Dean Masztak — 86

13. **N,J,O,C,** Tony Hunter — 85

14. **H,** Knute Rockne, no number

15. **A,D,E,** Derek Brown — 86

Fullbacks, Halfbacks, and All Other Backs

In the old days when football was a simple game, the big back who blocked was the fullback. The fast kid who carried the ball was the halfback. And that's the way it was for generations of Irish football. Now there are halfbacks, slotbacks, tailbacks, wingbacks, and more. A simple game of blocking and running has gotten complicated. This chapter looks at some of the many great backs who have represented the Irish on the gridiron.

Pick the Right Back

1. Which recent Notre Dame back surpassed George Gipp's record of 8.1 yards per carry over a season?

   A. Reggie Brooks
   B. Tony Brooks
   C. Jerome Bettis
   D. Robert Farmer

Ricky Watters was a controversial ND back in the early '90s.
(Photo by Bill Panzica)

2. Who holds the single-season rushing record for Notre Dame?

   A. Al Hunter
   B. Jerome Bettis
   C. Allen Pinkett
   D. Vagas Ferguson

3. Who holds the single-season record for most carries by a Notre Dame back?

   A. Vagas Ferguson
   B. Allen Pinkett
   C. Al Hunter
   D. Wayne Bullock

4. Who holds the single-game record for carries by an Irish back?

   A. Vagas Ferguson
   B. Allen Pinkett
   C. Jim Stone
   D. Phil Carter

5. Which of the following backs *did not* lead the Irish in rushing for three seasons?

   A. Emil "Red" Sitko
   B. George Gipp
   C. Allen Pinkett
   D. Christie Flanagan

6. Which of the following Irish backs did not lead the team in rushing for two seasons?

   A. Mark Green
   B. Vagas Ferguson
   C. Randy Kinder
   D. Jerome Bettis

7. Which Heisman Trophy winners also led the Irish in interceptions the year he won the trophy?

   A. Angelo Bertelli
   B. Paul Hornung
   C. Johnny Lattner
   D. John Lujack

8. Which defensive back leads Notre Dame in career interceptions?

   A. Nick Rassas
   B. Clarence Ellis
   C. Ralph Stepaniak
   D. Luther Bradley

9. This back also holds the record for the longest punt in Irish history.

   A. Joe Restic
   B. Nick Pietrosante
   C. Elmer Layden
   D. Bill Shakespeare

10. Which back is the all-time seasonal leader in kickoff re-
    turns?

    A. Nick Eddy
    B. Johnny Lattner
    C. Paul Castner
    D. Gary Diminick

11. This back holds the season record for most punt returns.

    A. Dave Duerson
    B. Tom Schoen
    C. Nick Rassas
    D. Todd Lyght

12. Which of these defensive backs did not lead the entire
    team in playing time for at least one season?

    A. Dave Duerson
    B. Todd Lyght
    C. Tom Carter
    D. Jeff Burris

13. Since 1960 only one defensive back has led the team in
    tackles for a season. Who is it?

    A. Dave Duerson
    B. Jeff Burris
    C. Rod Smith
    D. Brian Magee

True or False

1. _____ Tony Rice has more career rushing yards than Jerome Bettis.

2. _____ Lee Becton has more career rushing yards than Mark Green.

3. _____ The last Notre Dame back to go over 200 yards rushing in a game was Jerome Bettis.

4. _____ Vagas Ferguson is the only Notre Dame back to have more than one 200-yard game.

5. _____ Randy Kinder has more career rushing yards than Jerome Bettis.

6. _____ Of the top ten all-time rushers at Notre Dame, only one, Emil Sitko, is also in the top ten for longest run from scrimmage.

7. _____ George Gipp never averaged less than 40 yards per carry in a season.

8. _____ Allen Pinkett is the Notre Dame career scoring leader with 320 points.

9. _____ Pinkett also had the highest seasonal scoring totals.

10. _____ None of the seasons that produced the top ten seasonal rushers also produced a national championship.

Back Match

WHAT?	WHO?
1. This defensive back is the only player to lead ND in punt returns for four years.	**A.** Jeff Burris
2. He's the only Notre Dame back to lead the NCAA in rushing.	**B.** Ricky Watters
3. This back led the Irish in rushing and passing in 1935.	**C.** Allen Rossum
4. He is the most recent back to play both offense and defense in the same game.	**D.** Allen Pinkett
5. He has the longest punt return in Notre Dame history.	**E.** Shawn Wooden
6. In 1996 he set a Notre Dame record with two punt returns for touchdowns in one quarter.	**F.** Tom Gibbons
7. He was the only back who captained the 1995 team.	**G.** Rocky Bleier
8. This defensive back was a captain on Dan Devine's last team in 1980.	**H.** Bill Shakespeare
9. This back was the sole captain on the 1967 squad.	**I.** Creighton Miller
10. He was second in scoring in the entire NCAA for each of two consecutive seasons.	**J.** Dave Duerson

Answers to Pick the Right Back

1. **D:** Farmer lugged the pigskin 8.5 yards every time he touched the ball in the 1996 season. Reggie Brooks came close in 1992 with 8.0 years per carry.

2. **D:** Ferguson raced for 1,437 yards in 1979.

3. **D:** Ferguson carried an amazing 301 times in that same 1979 season.

4. **D:** Ferguson doesn't hold this one. Phil Carter ran the ball 40 times versus Michigan State in 1980.

5. **A:** Sitko did it an amazing four times.

6. **D:** Bettis only led the team in rushing in 1991. He had a great 1992 season, but that was Reggie Brooks's time to shine.

7. **D:** Unbelievably, every one of these players did lead Notre Dame in interceptions in one season. Lattner in fact did it twice. But only Lujack did it in the season he won the Heisman.

8. **D:** Bradley had 17 during his All-American career.

9. **D:** Shakespeare boomed an 86-yard punt in 1935 against Pittsburgh. All the other backs listed were also punters but none topped Shakespeare.

10. **C:** Castner had a 44.5-yard average way back in 1922. Lattner was close with 41.4 in 1953. Eddy hit 48.3 in 1966, but only had four returns, just short of the minimum number of returns needed to qualify.

11. **B:** Schoen had 43 in 1967. The closest since then is 34 by Tim Brown in 1987 and Dave Duerson in 1982.

12. **B:** The other three were all used extensively on special teams.

13. **D:** The unsung Magee had 81 tackles in 1994.

True or False
ANSWERS

1. **True.**

2. **True.**

3. **False.** It was Reggie Brooks versus USC in 1992.

4. **False.** Reggie Brooks did it twice in 1992 versus USC and Purdue.

5. **True.**

6. **True.** Allen Pinkett's long run against Dan Marino and Pitt didn't make the 81+ yard cutoff point.

7. **False.** Gipp had 63 carries for 244 yards or 3.9 per carry in 1917, his initial season.

8. **True.** Pinkett is the only nonkicker in the top five but he had 53 touchdowns.

9. **False.** Jerome Bettis topped Pinkett by two touchdowns less one Pinkett 2-point conversion.

10. **True.** Does this say something about the need for offensive balance?

Back Match

ANSWERS

1. **J,** Dave Duerson

2. **I,** Creighton Miller

3. **H,** Bill Shakespeare

4. **A,** Jeff Burris

5. **B,** Ricky Watters

6. **C,** Allen Rossum

7. **E,** Shawn Wooden

8. **F,** Tom Gibbons

9. **G,** Rocky Bleier

10. **D,** Allen Pinkett

George Gipp and the Four Horsemen

The legendary status of Notre Dame football is built on the twin pillars of George Gipp and the Four Horsemen. Gipp was a phenomenal athlete. His untimely death in 1920 made him an even more heroic figure. His deathbed speech, as depicted in *Knute Rockne, All-American,* can be recited verbatim by many ND loyalists. Here's how it was portrayed in the movie:

've got to go, Rock. It's all right. I'm not afraid. Some time, Rock, when the team is up against it, when things are wrong and the breaks are beating the boys—tell them to go in there with all they've got and win just one for the Gipper. I don't know where I'll be then, Rock. But I'll know about it, and I'll be happy.''

—ND Sports Information Dept.—Football Media Guide 1996

The Four Horsemen were created by Grantland Rice in 1924. Here is the text of that story:

utlined against a blue, gray October sky the Four Horsemen rode again. In dramatic lore they are known

HB Don Miller

FB Elmer Layden

HB Jim Crowley

QB Harry Stuhldreher

(Photo courtesy of University of Notre Dame Sports Information Dept.)

as famine, pestilence, destruction and death. These are only aliases. Their real names are Stuhldreher, Miller, Crowley and Layden. They formed the crest of the South Bend cyclone before which another fighting Army football team was swept over the precipice at the Polo Grounds yesterday afternoon as 55,000 spectators peered down on the bewildering panorama spread on the green plain below.

A cyclone can't be snared. It may be surrounded, but somewhere it breaks through to keep going. When the cyclone starts from South Bend, where the candle lights still gleam through the Indiana sycamores, those in the way must take to storm cellars at top speed. Yesterday the cyclone struck again, as Notre Dame beat Army 13 to 7, with a set of backfield stars that ripped and crashed through a strong Army defense with more speed and power than warring cadets could meet.

—Grantland Rice, *New York Herald Tribune*, October 19, 1924

Here's some trivia about these two legends of Notre Dame.

True or False

1. _____ None of the Four Horsemen ever captained a Notre Dame squad.

2. _____ George Gipp was Notre Dame's first consensus All-American.

3. _____ Gipp was involved in at least one touchdown each of his four years at Notre Dame.

4. _____ The Four Horsemen were the starting backfield in only the 1924 season, when they became famous.

5. _____ The Four Horsemen heard the "Win one for the Gipper" speech against Army.

6. _____ George Gipp planned to play baseball for the Chicago Cubs after he graduated from Notre Dame.

7. _____ George Gipp was Notre Dame's career leading rusher for over 55 years.

8. _____ All of the Four Horsemen became football coaches.

9. _____ Jim Crowley had the most career rushing yards of the Four Horsemen.

10. _____ Although the Four Horsemen are giants in football history, none stood taller than six feet and none weighed more than 162 pounds.

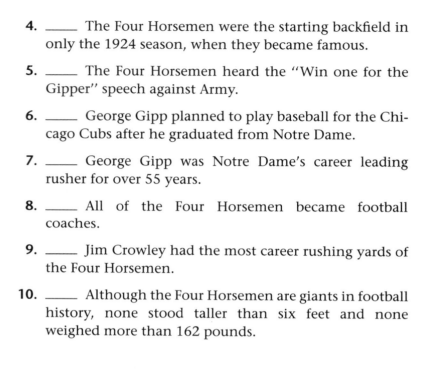

There is a stadium in the National Football League named for one of George Gipp's teammates. Do you know who he is?

In this era of corporate stadia, this may be difficult, so here's another hint: This stadium was originally built to be a replica of Notre Dame Stadium. Still don't know the answer? Here's one last hint: The player for whom this stadium is named was Gipp's fullback. Yes, Lambeau Field in Green Bay is named after Earl "Curly" Lambeau, who started the Packers and built that franchise. In many ways the Packers were modeled after Notre Dame; they had gold helmets and satin gold pants like Rockne's Irish. Only later did they add the big "G" to the previously unadorned helmet.

Lambeau Field has seen many additions since it was first built, but you can see the similarity to Notre Dame Stadium if you block out the sky boxes.

True or False
ANSWERS

1. **True.**

2. **True.**

3. **True.**

4. **False.** They started in 1923 and 1924.

5. **False.** The speech was against Army but it was not until 1928.

6. **True.** Gipp came to Notre Dame to play baseball and was spotted by Rockne drop-kicking the ball on campus.

7. **True.** Jerome Heavens surpassed him in 1978.

8. **True.** Jim Crowley at MSU and Fordham, Elmer Layden at Notre Dame, Don Miller at Georgia Tech, and Henry Stuhldreher at Wisconsin.

9. **False.** Don Miller had 1,933 and Crowley is second with 1,841 yards.

10. **True.**

Lou Holtz left Notre Dame second only to Knute Rockne in career victories.
(Photo by Bill Panzica)

Holtz

After five years of the Gerry Faust experiment, the Notre Dame administration had seen enough. Faust, a genuinely good person, was overmatched as a collegiate coach. He had been a high school coaching legend in Ohio at Cincinnati's Moeller High School. He had sent many of his best players to Notre Dame. But in the end, even with highly rated recruits, he could not put Notre Dame in the top echelon of college football, a place its fans believed was its destiny.

Since the lack of collegiate experience was the oft-cited reason for the Faust demise, the next head man needed to be one with significant collegiate experience. Enter Lou Holtz.

Luck of the Irish

WHERE THERE'S A WILL THERE'S A WAY

The volatile and energetic Holtz had always dreamed of a job with the Fighting Irish. Even though he had recently signed a five-year contract at the University of Minnesota, he left himself some room to maneuver. There were two clauses in his contract that would set him loose. One was if the Notre Dame job came open, and the other? A difficult task, but one Lou was up to. He had to take Minnesota to a bowl game, which he did in his second year. The Golden Gophers went to the Independence Bowl in Louisiana and Holtz went to the Golden Dome.

Holtz Highlights

1. Which of these players was not recruited by Holtz?

    A. Anthony Johnson
    B. Andy Heck
    C. Chris Zorich
    D. Pat Terrell

2. Which 1986 game does Holtz credit with turning around the team's attitude and serving as a springboard for future success?

    A. Michigan
    B. USC
    C. Michigan State
    D. Pittsburgh

3. That 1986 USC game also kicked off another Notre Dame drive. Which one?

   A. Steve Beuerlein's record-setting 1986 season
   B. Defensive line's streak of games with interceptions
   C. Tim Brown's 1987 Heisman campaign
   D. Rudy sold his movie after this game

4. This controversial call hurt Notre Dame in Holtz's first game, a loss to Michigan.

   A. Joel Williams's apparent touchdown being ruled a no-catch because he was out of bounds
   B. Mark Green's nonfumble on a late dive
   C. Stan Smagala being called for pass interference on Michigan's last scoring drive
   D. John Carney's field goal that was ruled wide but actually went over the upright

5. Who was Holtz's first quarterback at Notre Dame?

   A. Blair Kiel
   B. Scott Grooms
   C. Steve Beuerlein
   D. John Foley

6. Which of the following coaches did not coach under Holtz?

   A. Barry Alvarez
   B. Joe Yonto
   C. Ron Cooper
   D. Foge Fazio

7. Where did Holtz get his first head coaching position?

    A. William and Mary
    B. North Carolina State
    C. Arkansas
    D. The New York Jets

8. What brother combination became famous while playing for Holtz at NC State?

    A. Ty and Bill Barber
    B. Dave and Don Buckey
    C. Lawrence and Billy Taylor
    D. Bill and Cal Ripken

9. How many Notre Dame athletic directors did Holtz work with during his tenure?

    A. Two
    B. Three
    C. One
    D. Four

10. These three players were the college football "Three Amigos."

    A. Ricky Watters, Tony Brooks, Rocket Ismail
    B. Rick Mirer, Jerome Bettis, Lee Becton
    C. Frank Stams, Wes Pritchett, Mike Stonebreaker
    D. Jeff Burris, Tom Carter, Demetrius DuBose

11. Which of the following tight ends did not play for Lou Holtz?

A. Joel Williams
B. Mark Bavaro
C. Derek Brown
D. Irv Smith

12. What two Notre Dame players were featured on the covers of *Sports Illustrated College and Pro Football Preview* issues in 1987?

A. Mark Green and Dave Duerson
B. John Carney and Steve Beuerlein
C. Tim Brown and Joe Montana
D. Tim Brown and Mark Bavaro

Fighting Irish Factoid

EVEN THE GREATEST CAN'T WIN WITHOUT TALENT

Recruiting has always been a key to Notre Dame and Lou Holtz's success. His first recruiting coordinator, Vinny Cerrato, did a masterful job of bringing the nation's best to South Bend. Cerrato, now a head scout with the 49ers, signed the classes that led to the great teams in Holtz's early years. But even Cerrato made some mistakes. Can you name the offensive tackle who hailed from Colorado who wanted to attend Notre Dame in the worst way but was turned down? Here's a hint: He went on to start for archrival USC and was then the top draft choice of the Jacksonville Jaguars in their very first NFL draft and he made the Pro Bowl in 1997. Yes, tackle Tony Boselli.

Holtz's Heroes Scrambler

Match the Holtz player with the fact he is known for. The questions are in order but players names aren't.

WHAT?	WHO?
1. Knocked down the Miami 2-point conversion attempt, which sealed the Irish upset.	**A.** Ricky Watters
2. Returned two kickoffs for touchdowns at Michigan in 1989 to effectively win the game.	**B.** Reggie Ho
3. Leading rusher on 1988 national championship team.	**C.** Tim Brown
4. Lou Holtz's first Notre Dame kicker.	**D.** John Foley
5. Lou's first *USA Today* player-of-the-year recruit.	**E.** Pat Terrell
6. Won the 1988 Michigan game with 4 field goals.	**F.** John Carney
7. The one Heisman Trophy winner in Lou's tenure.	**G.** Mark Green
8. Was suspended for 1988 USC game for tardiness along with Tony Brooks.	**H.** Rocket Ismail

Holtz Highlight's
ANSWERS

1. **B:** Andy Heck, a tight end from Virginia, was actually a Gerry Faust recruit whom Holtz converted to an offensive tackle. Heck captained the 1988 national championship team.

2. **B:** The USC comeback capped by John Carney's winning field goal set the stage for a 1987 Cotton Bowl season and 1988 national championship.

3. **C:** Tim Brown's 252 all-purpose yardage was the highlight of the game and made him a favorite going into 1987 for the Heisman.

4. **A:** There was no luck of the Irish on this day. Although replays showed Williams was in bounds, the referee ruled otherwise.

5. **C:** Steve Beuerlein, a pure drop-back passer, was Holtz's 1986 quarterback.

6. **B:** Yonto, the longtime Notre Dame assistant, became an administrator under Holtz.

7. **A:** Although he coached at all these places, Holtz got his start at the Virginia school.

8. **B:** If you answered D, put this book down immediately and subscribe to *Baseball Weekly*.

9. **B:** Mike Wadsworth, Dick Rosenthal, and Gene Corrigan, who hired Holtz.

10. **C:** Stams, Pritchett, and Stonebreaker kept the 1988 champs loose and Holtz on guard for their pranks.

11. **B:** Bavaro was starring for the New York Giants by the time Holtz arrived at Notre Dame.

12. **D:** Not so fast on the Brown/Montana duo. Bavaro was coming off a Super Bowl win and Brown was "running" for the Heisman. It didn't hurt that Don Barr, *SI* publisher, was a Notre Dame grad either.

Holtz's Heroes Scrambler
ANSWERS

1. **E**, Pat Terrell

2. **H**, Rocket Ismail

3. **G**, Mark Green

4. **F**, John Carney

5. **D**, John Foley

6. **B**, Reggie Ho

7. **C**, Tim Brown

8. **A**, Ricky Watters

I

Inside Linebackers, Outside Linebackers, and Defensive Backs

Linebackers and defensive backs are the "skill players on the defensive side of the ball." They have many responsibilities from shedding blockers and supporting against the run to covering against the pass. As with all positions, Notre Dame has had its share of great ones. Here are some brain teasers about them.

Inside linebacker Greg Collins (#50), as seen here in the 1973 Sugar Bowl, was a defensive stalwart for the Irish in the mid-seventies.
(Photo courtesy of Willie Fry & the South Bend Tribune*)*

By the Numbers

Match the player with his uniform number.

1. Mike Townsend	**A.** 36
2. Bob Crable	**B.** 9
3. Tom Schoen	**C.** 60
4. Ted Burgmeier	**D.** 54
5. Jeff Burris	**E.** 58
6. Jim Lynch	**F.** 18
7. Steve Heimkreiter	**G.** 43
8. Mike Whittington	**H.** 27
9. Greg Collins	**I.** 27
10. Lyron Cobbins	**J.** 34
11. Nick Rassas	**K.** 42
12. Jerry Groom	**L.** 2
13. Bobby Taylor	**M.** 50
14. Todd Lyght	**N.** 7
15. Mike Stonebreaker	**O.** 61
16. John Pergine	**P.** 27
17. Mike McGill	**Q.** 50
18. Ned Bolcar	**R.** 1
19. Wes Pritchett	**S.** 50
20. Kinnon Tatum	**T.** 47

Multiple Choice

1. Who holds the record for most tackles in a career?

    A. Bob Golic
    B. Greg Collins
    C. Bob Crable
    D. Steve Heimkreiter

2. Who holds the record for most fumbles recovered in a season?

    A. Pat Terrell
    B. Tony Furjanic
    C. Mark Zavagnin
    D. Cedric Figaro

3. Who led the 1988 national championship team in tackles?

    A. Mike Stonebreaker
    B. Pat Terrell
    C. Wes Pritchett
    D. Todd Lyght

4. Who led the 1977 national champions in tackles?

    A. Joe Restic
    B. Bob Golic
    C. Steve Heimkreiter
    D. Bob Crable

5. Which defensive back was not also a quarterback?

   A. Todd Lyght
   B. Tom Schoen
   C. Ted Burgmeier
   D. Joe Restic

6. Who holds the career record for passes broken up, a statistic kept since 1956?

   A. Luther Bradley
   B. Todd Lyght
   C. Clarence Ellis
   D. Mike Townsend

7. Who has the most interceptions in a season since Mike Townsend set the season record in 1972 with 10?

   A. Bobby Taylor
   B. Pat Terrell
   C. Dave Duerson
   D. Todd Lyght

8. Who was the first player to lead Notre Dame in interceptions?

   A. Curly Lambeau
   B. Elmer Layden
   C. Creighton Miller
   D. George Gipp

Matches

Match the player with the feat.

WHAT?	WHO?
1. This defensive back played on the '88 national champions and the 1996 Carolina Panthers team that won the NFC West.	**A.** Nick Buoniconti
2. He has interceptions in each of his four seasons of eligibility and is the Notre Dame career interception leader.	**B.** Bobby Taylor
3. This defensive back made the fourth-down, goal-line stop against Richie Anderson of Penn State in 1992 that became immortalized as "Irish Impact."	**C.** Demetrius DuBose
4. This linebacker climbed the backs of his teammates to block a last-second Michigan field goal and preserve victory in 1979.	**D.** Dave Duerson
5. This linebacker led the 1995 squad in interceptions.	**E.** Bobby Leopold
6. This defensive back, currently a Washington Redskin, had the longest interception return of the Holtz era.	**F.** Jim Lynch

WHAT?	WHO?
7. This defensive back who later played for the Bears, Giants, and Cardinals had the longest interception return of the Faust era.	**G.** Lyron Cobbins
8. This linebacker was the heart of the Dolphins defense during their championship seasons of the mid-seventies.	**H.** Bob Crable
9. This linebacker was a second-round draft choice of the Tampa Bay Buccaneers in 1993.	**I.** Tom Carter
10. This linebacker earned a Super Bowl ring with the 49ers in their first Super Bowl victory in 1982.	**J.** Luther Bradley
11. This is the only Notre Dame captain to have played at LB or DB and to have won both a national championship in college and a Super Bowl in the pros.	**K.** Jeff Burris
12. This cornerback left Notre Dame early and became a second-round draft choice of the Philadelphia Eagles.	**L.** Pat Terrell

By the Numbers
ANSWERS

1. Mike Townsend, 27
2. Bob Crable, 43
3. Tom Schoen, 7
4. Ted Burgmeier, 18
5. Jeff Burris, 9
6. Jim Lynch, 61
7. Steve Heimkreiter, 58
8. Mike Whittington, 54
9. Greg Collins, 50
10. Lyron Cobbins, 36

11. Nick Rassas, 27
12. Jerry Groom, 50
13. Bobby Taylor, 27
14. Todd Lyght, 1
15. Mike Stonebreaker, 42
16. John Pergine, 50
17. Mike McGill, 60
18. Ned Bolcar, 47
19. Wes Pritchett, 34
20. Kinnon Tatum, 2

Multiple Choice
ANSWERS

1. **C:** Crable had 521 tackles over his four-year career.
2. **D:** Figaro recovered seven in Holtz's first season, 1986.
3. **C:** Pritchett has 112 tackles, Stonebreaker was second with 104.
4. **C:** Heimkreiter had 160, Golic had 152.
5. **A:** Lyght was a receiver/DB combination.

6. **C**: Ellis knocked away 32 passes during the 1969–71 seasons. Bradley is second with 27.

7. **D**: Lyght had 8 in 1989; Duerson had 7 in 1982.

8. **D**: Who else!

Matching
ANSWERS

1. **L**, Pat Terrell

2. **J**, Luther Bradley

3. **K**, Jeff Burris

4. **H**, Bob Crable

5. **G**, Lyron Cobbins

6. **I**, Tom Carter

7. **D**, Dave Duerson

8. **A**, Nick Buoniconti

9. **C**, Demetrius DuBose

10. **E**, Bobby Leopold

11. **F**, Jim Lynch

12. **B**, Bobby Taylor

Joe Montana became an even greater legend after he entered the NFL.
(Photo by Brother Charles McBride)

Joe Montana

He is arguably the most celebrated player in Notre Dame football history. Yet most of his recognition came after he graduated from ND. Although he led his team to a national championship and a dizzying number of comebacks, he was neither an All-American nor a first-round draft choice.

Joe Montana sounded like a star player the first time you heard his name, but he had to wait for his chance to shine at Notre Dame. Now he's a football legend. In South Bend he was viewed as a good game player who didn't care much for practice.

Montana Multiple Choice

1. What nickname did Joe earn during his collegiate days?

   A. The Ringgold Rifle
   B. Broadway Joe
   C. Big Time
   D. The Comeback Kid

2. What previous Notre Dame quarterback wore Joe's #3?

   A. Terry Hanratty
   B. John Huarte
   C. Tom Clements
   D. Coley O'Brien

3. Montana was also recruited to play this sport at the collegiate level.

   A. Baseball
   B. Basketball
   C. Track
   D. Ice hockey

4. Which of these quarterbacks was drafted ahead of Montana in the 1979 draft?

   A. Jack Thompson
   B. Phil Simms
   C. Steve Fuller
   D. All of the above

5. How many games did Montana start as quarterback in the 1977 national championship season?

   A. All 11 plus bowl
   B. 10 plus bowl
   C. 9 plus bowl
   D. 8 plus bowl

6. Who were the two quarterbacks ahead of Montana on the early season 1977 depth chart?

   A. Tim Koegel and Mike Courey
   B. Cliff Brown and Frank Allocco
   C. Rusty Lisch and Gary Forystek
   D. Rusty Lisch and Tom Burgmeier

7. What did Montana's first wife, Kim, do while he was at Notre Dame?

   A. Worked at St. Joe Bank
   B. Worked at Bazney Ford
   C. Worked in the Sports Information Department
   D. Worked in the Placement Office

8. What did the Notre Dame doctors give Montana to fight off flu symptoms when he was taken into the locker room during the Notre Dame–Houston Cotton Bowl in 1979?

   A. OTC flu medicine
   B. Nondrowsy cold medicine
   C. Chicken soup
   D. Decongestants

9. Who caught the winning score in that fabled Houston comeback?

   A. Tom Domin
   B. Ken MacAfee
   C. Kris Haines
   D. Vagas Ferguson

10. What other big pass had Haines caught that season?

    A. Winning score against Michigan
    B. Only touchdown against Missouri
    C. "Hail Mary" pass against Pitt.
    D. Bomb that led comeback against USC

11. This Notre Dame player, a member of the 1988 national championship team, played with Joe for the Kansas City Chiefs.
    A. Anthony Johnson
    B. Tim Grunhard
    C. Andy Heck
    D. Pat Terrell

Red Shirt Year

Montana entered Notre Dame in 1974, yet stayed for five seasons. The Irish had a policy against "red-shirting" at that time. Do you know what allowed his extra season? A shoulder injury kept him out during the 1976 season, so he petitioned and was granted an extra year of eligibility, the 1978 season.

Montana Matchups

MATCHUP	WHO?
1. This Notre Dame All-American and favorite Montana target was with San Francisco when they drafted Montana.	A. Bob Golic
2. This ND player was drafted before Montana in 1979.	B. Terry Eurick
3. This ND quarterback split time with Joe in the 1975 season.	C. Ken MacAfee

MATCHUP	WHO?
4. This ND player was also drafted before Montana in 1979.	**D.** Rich Slager
5. This is the player Bill Walsh wanted to be his quarterback in the 1979 draft.	**E.** Ted Burgmeier
6. This player was on the receiving end of "The Catch" that put the 49ers into their first Super Bowl.	**F.** Dave Huffman
7. This Notre Dame teammate was an opponent in Joe's first Super Bowl.	**G.** Phil Simms
8. This ND player who later became a defensive back caught an 84-yard Montana touchdown to lead the comeback against North Carolina.	**H.** Ross Browner
9. After the January 1, 1978, Cotton Bowl win against Texas, this player was on the cover of *Sports Illustrated*.	**I.** Dwight Clark

Out of the Shotgun
THE COMEBACK THAT WASN'T

Montana's athletic prowess was not limited to the gridiron. What campus event did Montana win during his career?

ND–USC 1978. Notre Dame followed up their 1977 national championship by getting off to a rocky start with consecutive home losses to Missouri and Michigan. They then ripped off eight straight wins and headed to LA to face the dreaded Trojans. Trailing in the first half, Montana led a stirring comeback that gave the Irish a 24–22 lead. But, after a controversial non-call on a Paul McDonald fumble, the Trojans kicked a game-winning field goal. Irish tears flowed on the field and in the stands, where the senior class had joined the team. But Montana turned the trip home into a positive. How? He met the woman who was to become his second wife, Cass. She was a stewardess working for United Airlines on the charter the team took back to Chicago.

True or False

1. _____ Montana is the only 1970s starting quarterback to come from western Pennsylvania, a noted quarterback breeding ground.

2. _____ In 1975, Dan Devine preferred Rick Slager to Montana because he performed better in practice.

3. _____ Dan Devine recruited Montana with the idea of using his athletic ability as wide receiver.

4. _____ Montana's lack of playing time in 1977 led to Devine's parking space being painted over at the football offices.

5. _____ Montana's #3 was temporarily retired until Rick Mirer asked for it when he was being recruited.

6. _____ The reason the 49ers picked Montana in the third

round in 1979 is that Eddie DeBartolo, a Notre Dame grad, liked him.

7. _____ Montana started right away for the 49ers.

8. _____ Montana chose #16 with the 49ers because #3 was taken.

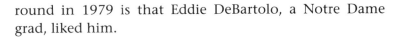

Commercial Exposure

Although Joe Montana is a take-charge guy on the football field, he was actually rather shy off it. He met his third wife, and mother of his four children, Jennifer, on the set of a television commercial shoot. What did Jennifer do to get Joe's attention? The director was concerned that Joe was up-tight and not performing as they wanted him to. So the director asked Jennifer, the female lead in the commercial, to pinch Joe's backside. Joe relaxed, the shoot was a success, and a long-lasting romance blossomed.

Joe Montana's Top Five Comebacks

Just in case you didn't think he'd been doing it all his life.

1. 1979 Cotton Bowl vs. Houston—It's amazing what chicken soup can do; ND won 35–34.

2. 1977 Purdue game—Third-stringer, Montana comes off the bench to lead the rally that beat the Boilermakers 31–24 and started the national championship drive.

3. 1978 USC game—Though Notre Dame eventually lost 27–25 on a last-second field goal, Montana's heroics getting them a late lead are memorable.

4. 1975 Air Force—Before Gerry Faust had his Air Force blues, Dan Devine almost had his in Colorado Springs. Montana drove ND to three fourth-quarter scores to pull out a 31–30 win.

5. 1976 North Carolina—The Tar Heels were ready to celebrate with a 14–7 lead but Montana pulled out another victory with two late scores.

Montana Multiple Choice
ANSWERS

1. **D:** From Air Force in 1975 to the Houston Cotton Bowl in January 1979, comebacks were Montana's specialty.

2. **D:** O'Brien, the hero of the 1966 national championship, also wore #3. Hanratty wore #5, Clements #2, and Huarte #7.

3. **B:** Montana had scholarship offers to ACC powers Maryland and NC State.

4. **D:** All of the above. Thompson by Cincinnati, Simms by the Giants, Fuller by Kansas City.

5. **D:** Montana was the third-string quarterback until an injury put him into the Purdue game, where he led Notre Dame to a comeback win.

6. **C:** Lisch started the Pittsburgh win and Mississippi loss and was pulled from the Purdue game. Forystek was driving the Irish downfield but injured on a scramble by

Purdue linebacker Fred Arrington. The rest, as they say, is history!

7. **C:** Kim assisted Roger Valdiserri and the rest of the Sports Information Department.

8. **C:** Yes, grandmother's recipe works just fine.

9. **C:** Kris Haines caught the "out" pattern in the right corner of the end zone.

10. **D:** Notre Dame lost all of the above games except Pitt.

11. **B:** Grunhard was Montana's center while Joe was with the Chiefs.

Montana Matchup
ANSWERS

1. **C,** Ken MacAfee

2. **A,** Bob Golic

3. **D,** Rich Slager

4. **F,** Dave Huffman

5. **G,** Phil Simms

6. **H,** Ross Browner

7. **I,** Dwight Clark

8. **E,** Ted Burgmeier

9. **B,** Terry Eurick

Out of the Shotgun
ANSWER

Joe won a slam-dunk contest during the Bookstore Basketball tournament.

True or False
ANSWERS

1. **False.** Tom Clements was from McKees Rocks, PA, in the same area.

2. **True.** Montana seemed to work his magic exclusively in games.

3. **False.** Dan Devine did not recruit Montana. He was part of Ara Parseghian's last recruiting class.

4. **False.** The loss to Mississippi in game 2 of the 1977 season led to that ugly incident.

5. **False.** They were just saving it for a special player.

6. **False.** Although it is the subject of some debate, either Tony Randazzo, the head 49ers scout, or Bill Walsh, the head coach, wanted him.

7. **False.** Steve Deberg, who would go on to be unseated by the likes of John Elway and Steve Young later in his career, initially started ahead of Montana.

8. **False.** The NFL mandated at that time that #3 was for kickers only.

Kickers, Punters, and Kick Returners

The kicking game has been a strong part of Notre Dame's gridiron history. Some players are longtime contributors in this area while others are in the spotlight for only a brief moment. Either way, many of them have become part of Irish football lore.

Multiple Choice

1. Which punter leads Notre Dame in career punting average?

    A. Blair Kiel
    B. Joe Restic
    C. Hunter Smith
    D. Craig Hentrich

Willie Fry blocking a Northwestern punt
(Photo courtesy of Willie Fry & the South Bend Tribune*)*

2. Ranked just behind Hentrich is another Holtz-era punter. Who is he?

   A. Brian Ford
   B. Dan Sorensen
   C. Jim Sexton
   D. Vince Phelan

3. Only one player ranks in the top five in both punting and interceptions for a career at Notre Dame. Can you name him?

   A. Joe Restic
   B. Vince Phelan
   C. Nick Rassas
   D. Tom MacDonald

4. Only one player ranks in the top five in both punting and passing for a career at Notre Dame. Can you name him?

   A. Paul Hornung
   B. Blair Kiel
   C. George Gipp
   D. Hunter Smith

5. Which kicker made the famous 51-yard field goal against Michigan in 1980 when the wind miraculously stopped in Notre Dame Stadium?

   A. Dave Reeve
   B. Chuck Male
   C. Mike Johnston
   D. Harry Oliver

6. Who is the career field goal leader at Notre Dame?

   A. Dave Reeve
   B. John Carney
   C. Craig Hentrich
   D. Harry Oliver

7. Who has the longest field goal in Notre Dame history?

   A. Dave Reeve
   B. John Carney
   C. Craig Hentrich
   D. Harry Oliver

8. Through the 1996 season, who was the last kicker to lead Notre Dame in scoring?

   A. Craig Hentrich
   B. John Carney
   C. Kevin Pendergast
   D. Reggie Ho

9. How many extra points did Notre Dame miss in the 1996 season?

   A. Two
   B. Four
   C. Six
   D. Eight

10. Who holds the record for most points in a game by a kicker at Notre Dame and what team did he do it against?

   A. Craig Hentrich—Miami 1990
   B. Scott Hempel—USC 1970
   C. Dave Reeve—Georgia Tech 1977
   D. Kevin Pendergast—Navy 1993

11. Which kicker beat Michigan with four field goals in 1988?

    A. Craig Hentrich
    B. Reggie Ho
    C. John Carney
    D. Mike Johnston

12. Which member of the Four Horsemen also had 88 career punt returns?

    A. Jim Crowley
    B. Harry Stuhldreher
    C. Don Miller
    D. Elmer Layden

13. Who holds the record for most kickoff returns in a single game?

    A. Rocket Ismail
    B. Mark McLane
    C. Tim Brown
    D. George Gipp

14. Who holds the season record for kickoff return yardage?

    A. Tim Brown
    B. Paul Hornung
    C. Rocket Ismail
    D. Jim Stone

15. How many times did the Rocket take two kicks back for touchdowns in one game?

    A. None
    B. One
    C. Two
    D. Three

16. Who holds the record for most kick returns (punts and kickoffs) for touchdowns in a career?

    A. Ricky Watters
    B. Nick Rassas
    C. Tim Brown
    D. Rocket Ismail

True or False

1. ____ Craig Hentrich holds the top three season records in punting.

2. ____ Notre Dame kickers have made all their extra points in only six seasons.

3. ____ No Notre Dame player has made all of his extra points in more than one season.

4. ____ The most extra points ever attempted in a single game by a Notre Dame team was in 1900 against a high school team.

5. ____ Gus Dorais, Knute Rockne's quarterback, was also a kicker and ranks fourth in PATs attempted in a career.

6. ____ The holder for the crucial missed extra point against USC in 1996 was Ron Powlus and not regular holder Hunter Smith.

7. ____ Allen Rossum tied the Notre Dame record for punt returns for touchdowns in a career with three in 1996.

8. ____ Rossum was the only Notre Dame player to score on a punt return in 1996.

9. _____ George Gipp is the highest ranking player in average return yard (punts and kickoffs) prior to 1970.

10. _____ Joe Restic punted five times and averaged over 50 yards per punt in 1975 vs. Air Force.

By the Numbers

Match these kickers and returners with their uniform number (two are same number).

1. Ricky Watters	**A.** 27
2. Rocket Ismail	**B.** 52
3. Tim Brown	**C.** 90
4. Craig Hentrich	**D.** 15
5. John Carney	**E.** 42
6. Dave Reeve	**F.** 13
7. Joe Restic	**G.** 7
8. Bob Thomas	**H.** 98
9. Jim Stone	**I.** 8
10. Allen Rossum	**J.** 12
11. Joe Azzaro	**K.** 81
12. Scott Hempel	**L.** 25
13. Nick Rassas	**M.** 12

Multiple Choice
ANSWERS

1. **D:** Hentrich leads with a whopping 44.1 yard average.

2. **D:** Vince Phelan averaged 40.9 in 1987. Hunter Smith could supplant Phelan before he graduates.

3. **A:** Restic was a four-year punter and three-year starter at safety in the late 70s.

4. **B:** Kiel handled the punting duties from 1980–1983 and averaged 40.67 yards per punt. He also ranks fourth in career completions.

5. **D:** It's still referred to as the "Legend of Harry O": 51 yards on the last play of the game and if the wind hadn't stopped . . . who knows?

6. **B:** Carney booted 51 career field goals for the Irish. Hentrich and Reeve are tied for second at 39.

7. **A:** Reeve hit one for 53 yards against Pittsburgh in 1976.

8. **C:** Pendergast had 87 point to lead the 1993 team.

9. **D:** Jim Sanson missed six and Scott Palumbo and Chris McCarthy missed one each.

10. **A:** Hard to believe that such a record would be set against Miami, but Hentrich had 5 FGs and 2 PATs for 17 points.

11. **B:** Reggie Ho went four for four to start the 1988 season off with a big win.

12. **B:** Quarterback and punt returner. Not a combination we would likely see today.

13. **D:** Gipp returned 10 versus Army in 1920.

14. **C:** Rocket averaged 29.5 yards per return in 1988.

15. **C:** He did it against Michigan in 1989 and Rice in 1988.

16. **C & D:** They are tied with six each.

True or False
ANSWERS

1. **True.** And his fourth season, 1991, ranks fifth.

2. **True.** It seems so easy on TV, doesn't it?

3. **False.** Craig Hentrich did it in 1990 and 1991.

4. **True.** Frank Winters tried 12 PATs, converting 9, during a game against Englewood High School in 1900. Who put the schedule together back then?

5. **True.** They were much more versatile back then.

6. **True.** Strange but true.

7. **True.** He may make this record his own in 1997.

8. **False.** Autry Denson scored against Pittsburgh in addition to Rossum's two scores that day.

9. **True.** He averaged 17.7 yards per return . . . amazing.

10. **True.** Restic hit 5 punts for 258 yards.

Match the Numbers
ANSWERS

1. **M, J,** Ricky Watters, 12

2. **L,** Rocket Ismail, 25

3. **K,** Tim Brown, 81

4. **M, J,** Craig Hentrich, 12

5. **I,** John Carney, 8

6. **F,** Dave Reeve, 13

7. **G,** Joe Restic, 7

8. **H,** Bob Thomas, 98

9. **E,** Jim Stone, 42

10. **D,** Allen Rossum, 15

11. **C,** Joe Azzaro, 90

12. **B,** Scott Hempel, 52

13. **A,** Nick Rassas, 27

Leahy

Frank Leahy is always the second name that comes to mind when one discusses Notre Dame football coaches. Rockne lit the football torch in South Bend and Leahy picked it up. Part of the reason for this is that he was the second coach to "win" a national title while at Notre Dame. Leahy was an intense coach whose commitment to excellence won the respect of his charges. Leahy's "lads" have stayed close throughout the years, a tribute to the team spirit he instilled.

Frank Leahy Multiple Choice

1. Leahy's winning percentage at Notre Dame is second only to Rockne's. Which percentage is it?

    A. .881
    B. .855
    C. .821
    D. .781

Coach Leahy had the second-highest winning percentage in NCAA history.
(Photo courtesy of University of Notre Dame Sports Information Dept.)

2. Which of the following coaches lost the fewest games while at Notre Dame?

   A. Rockne
   B. Leahy
   C. Parseghian
   D. Holtz

3. Leahy spent his early years in what town?

   A. Boston, MA
   B. Omaha, NE
   C. Cicus, IL
   D. Winner, SD

4. Which college did Frank Leahy attend?

   A. Notre Dame
   B. Holy Cross
   C. Fordham
   D. Boston College

5. What position did Leahy play in college?

   A. Quarterback
   B. Halfback
   C. End
   D. Tackle

6. Which college(s) did Leahy *not* coach at?

   A. Holy Cross
   B. Boston College
   C. Fordham
   D. Michigan State

7. Which of the following legendary NFL coaches was one of Leahy's prize pupils?

   A. Paul Brown
   B. George Halas
   C. Vince Lombardi
   D. John Madden

8. Which of the following coaches *did not* coach 11 seasons at Notre Dame?

   A. Leahy
   B. Parseghian
   C. Holtz
   D. None of the above

9. Leahy coached his first game at Notre Dame against an old coaching colleague. Who was it?

   A. Jim Crowley
   B. Biggie Munn
   C. Miles Casteil
   D. Duffy Daugherty

10. How many games had Leahy been coaching at Notre Dame before one of his squads lost?

   A. Four
   B. Six
   C. Eight
   D. Ten

11. After Leahy returned from the service in 1945, how many games did his teams lose for the rest of the 40s?

    A. None
    B. One
    C. Two
    D. Three

12. How many seasons did Leahy miss due to his service in WWII and how many coaches did Notre Dame have during that time?

    A. One season—one coach
    B. Two seasons—one coach
    C. Two seasons—two coaches
    D. Three seasons—two coaches

True or False

1. _____ Rockne coached more Heisman winners than Leahy.

2. _____ Leahy could be called the "Catholic school coach" because he was an assistant at Georgetown and Fordham and a head coach at Boston College and Notre Dame.

3. _____ No Leahy team was ever outscored over the course of a season.

4. _____ Frank Leahy never coached Notre Dame in a bowl game.

5. _____ Leahy had an "escape clause" in his Boston College contract that would let him come to Notre Dame.

6. ____ Leahy provides linkage between Rockne and Lombardi.

7. ____ Leahy's first practice session as coach in 1941 was on St. Patrick's Day.

8. ____ Leahy is the only coach affiliated with both the Four Horsemen and Fordham's "Seven Blocks of Granite."

9. ____ Terry Brennan, Leahy's successor, coached line for him.

10. ____ Leahy has the record of consecutive wins at Notre Dame with 21.

11. ____ Before Frank Leahy moved him up the depth chart, future Heisman winner Angelo Bertelli was on the seventh team.

12. ____ In Leahy's day it was the coaches who went one-on-one with the players.

13. ____ Leahy leads all Notre Dame coaches with six two-time All-Americans.

14. ____ Frank Leahy never coached anywhere in a bowl game.

Leahy's Lads Matchups

Match the players with something they are noted for.

WHAT?	WHO?
1. This player was Leahy's first consensus All-American and later coached Bob Davie, Lou Holtz's successor, at Youngstown State.	**A.** Jerry Croon
2. This starting quarterback in 1948 had a son who later was a basketball All-American for Notre Dame.	**B.** Leon Hart
3. He was the right tackle on the 1946–47 teams although he weighed in at only 213 pounds and stood just 6 feet tall.	**C.** George Connor
4. The starting quarterback in 1949 had great bloodlines; his son played for Holtz at Minnesota and was a first-round draft choice by the New York Giants in 1989.	**D.** John Yonakor
5. This 1943 end also had great bloodlines even though Digger Phelps didn't recognize them. His son played for Dean Smith at North Carolina.	**E.** Frank Tripucka
6. This center/linebacker was captain of the 1950 squad and a consensus All-American.	**F.** Bob Williams

WHAT?	WHO?
7. This tackle was the 1946 Outland Trophy winner and later a voice of Notre Dame football.	**G.** Ziggy Czarobski
8. He was the last lineman to win the Heisman Trophy and even won the 1949 AP male athlete of the year.	**H.** Bob Dove

Multiple Choice
ANSWERS

1. **B:** Amazingly .855.

2. **B:** Leahy lost one fewer game than Rockne, who coached for two more seasons.

3. **D:** Leahy was the "winner from Winner."

4. **A:** He was an early "double domer" in the career sense.

5. **D:** Leahy was a tough lineman under Rockne.

6. **A:** Leahy followed Crowley of Four Horsemen fame to Michigan State and Fordham and was then named head coach at Boston College.

7. **C:** Lombardi learned under Leahy while at Fordham.

8. **D:** Eleven seems to be the magic number for the most successful Notre Dame coaches since Rockne.

9. **C:** They were assistants together at Michigan State in the 1930s.

10. **D:** Yes, his 1941 Notre Dame team was 8–0–1 and he opened the 1942 season with a tie against Wisconsin before losing to Georgia Tech.

11. **A:** Four seasons with no losses and just two measly ties. One of these two was the famous 0–0 tie at Yankee Stadium in New York versus Army.

12. **C:** Ed McKeever's team was 8–2 in 1944 and Hugh Devore's was 7–2–1 in 1945.

True or False
ANSWERS

1. **False.** There was no Heisman Trophy in Rockne's time.

2. **True.**

3. **False.** The 4–4–1 team of 1950 was outscored 139–140.

4. **True.** The Irish skipped bowls from Rockne's time until 1970.

5. **False.** He had a verbal commitment that would allow him to take the Notre Dame job if it became open.

6. **True.** Rockne recruited and coached Leahy, who in turn coached Lombardi.

7. **True.** Sounds like there's something to this destiny thing.

8. **False.** Crowley was one of the Four Horsemen and was the head coach of the "Seven Blocks of Granite." Leahy was still in high school when "the Horsemen rode against a blue, gray October sky."

9. **False.** He was the freshman coach.

10. **False.** He had it until Holtz broke it with 23 in 1988–1989.

11. **True.** All great coaches know how to spot and successfully use talent.

12. **True,** and they didn't even wear pads.

13. **True.**

14. **False.** He led Boston College to a Sugar Bowl win over Tennessee in 1940.

Leahy's Lads Matchups
ANSWERS

1. **H,** Bob Dove

2. **E,** Frank Tripucka

3. **G,** Ziggy Czarobski

4. **F,** Bob Williams

5. **D,** John Yonakor

6. **A,** Jerry Croon

7. **C,** George Connor

8. **B,** Leon Hart

Movies, Television, and Press Coverage

Notre Dame has always been a darling of the media. The name is magic both in terms of drawing power for audiences and a suspension of sentiment that would otherwise make certain situations seem corny. Notre Dame home games are broadcast nationally and most road games are as well. Movies have been made about some of Notre Dame's most famous figures and even a previously unknown, except on campus, walk-on. Here are some tidbits about the star power of Notre Dame.

Multimedia Multiple Choice

1. Of the top six college games from a television ratings standpoint of all time, how many has Notre Dame been involved in?

   A. Three
   B. Four
   C. Five
   D. Six

Knute Rockne was on his way to make an instructional film when his plane crashed in Bazaar, Kansas.
(Photo courtesy of University of Notre Dame Sports Information Dept.)

2. What is the highest rated televised football game of all time?

    A. ND–Michigan State 10–10 tie 1966
    B. ND–USC   55–24 SC win 1974
    C. ND–USC   21–21 tie 1968
    D. ND–Texas   38–10 Cotton Bowl win 1978

3. Who played George Gipp in the movie *Knute Rockne, All-American*?

    A. Gipp himself
    B. Gerald Ford
    C. Ronald Reagan
    D. Pat O'Brien

4. Who played the title role of Rockne in that film?

    A. Gerald Ford
    B. Pat O'Brien
    C. Clark Gable
    D. James Dean

5. *Knute Rockne, All-American* premiered in:

    A. Chicago
    B. Hollywood
    C. Laurium, Michigan
    D. South Bend

6. Of the three highest rated games from a television standpoint since 1988, how many has Notre Dame been in?

    A. Zero
    B. One
    C. Two
    D. Three

7. What is the highest rated televised game since 1988?

   A. 1989 Miami 27–10 win over Notre Dame
   B. 1988 Irish 31–30 win over Miami
   C. 1993 ND 31–24 win over Florida State
   D. 1989 ND 34–24 win over Penn State

8. What is the only non–Notre Dame game among the top six in television ratings of all time?

   A. Michigan–OSU 1972
   B. USC–UCLA 1968
   C. Oklahoma–Nebraska 1971
   D. Auburn–Alabama 1978

9. The city in which the movie *Rudy* premiered is:

   A. Joliet, Illinois, Rudy's hometown
   B. Chicago
   C. Hollywood
   D. South Bend

10. Who played the lead in the movie *Rudy?*

    A. James Woods
    B. Michael J. Fox
    C. Sean Astin
    D. Matthew Perry

11. For which network(s) did Ara Parseghian broadcast after his retirement from coaching?

    A. ABC
    B. CBS
    C. NBC
    D. ESPN
    E. All of the above
    F. A & B
    G. A & C

True or False

1. _____ The writing team that produced *Rudy* is the same team that did the movie *Hoosiers.*

2. _____ Sean Astin is the son of Patty Duke Astin.

3. _____ Rudy is the only player to be carried off the field at Notre Dame Stadium.

4. _____ Rudy didn't really get a sack like they showed in the movie.

5. _____ The players didn't really turn in their jerseys to Devine to protest Rudy not dressing for Georgia Tech.

6. _____ Even though it didn't affect the national title picture, the Notre Dame–FSU Orange Bowl was the highest rated bowl game following the 1995 season.

7. _____ The highest rated bowl game since 1988 is the January 1989 Fiesta Bowl victory versus West Virginia to win the national title.

8. _____ Norm from *Cheers,* actor George Wendt, spoke at the pep rally before the final Notre Dame–Miami game in 1990.

9. _____ Knute Rockne was a spokesperson for Studebaker.

10. _____ *Rudy* scenes were filmed at halftime of an actual game in 1992 versus Boston College.

11. _____ Former All-American defensive back Luther Bradley was a commentator on Notre Dame games for Mutual radio.

12. ____ Notre Dame is the only professional or college team to have its football games broadcast nationally on radio.

13. ____ Despite all the Notre Dame alumni involved in broadcasting, none besides Bradley has done the games on the Mutual/Westwood One Network.

14. ____ Regis Philbin, of *Regis and Kathy Lee* fame, is a Notre Dame alumnus and a huge fan of the Irish.

Multimedia Multiple Choice
ANSWERS

1. **C:** Unbelievable but true. The Irish could be dubbed "National Ratings Champions."

2. **C:** One of the less recognized games, it still pulled a 22.9 rating, meaning almost one in four homes in America tuned in.

3. **C:** Why do you think they call him the Gipper?

4. **B:** O'Brien was a star actor at that time.

5. **D:** It's a moment the old-timers always referred to in South Bend.

6. **D:** Again, hard to believe but true.

7. **C:** #1 vs. #2 drew a lot of viewers.

8. **C:** Another #1 vs. #2 pulled big numbers.

9. **D:** Biggest excitement since the *Rockne* premier.

10. **C.**

11. **F:** He even did Notre Dame games on air!

True or False
ANSWERS

1. **True.** They've got heartwarming sports stories down.

2. **True.** And John Astin of *The Addams Family* is his father.

3. **True.**

4. **False.** He really did that in his 27 seconds of action.

5. **True.** Devine was inaccurately portrayed to build some conflict into the movie.

6. **False.** The Northwestern–USC Rose Bowl topped the Nebraska–Florida national championship game in the Fiesta Bowl in terms of rating. The Orange Bowl came in third.

7. **False.** That game is well down the list with a rating of 15.0.

8. **True.** He attended Notre Dame before pursuing an acting career.

9. **True.** Knute was ahead of his time.

10. **True.** Maybe they should have waited a year. They needed the inspiration in the 1993 game.

11. **True.** Luther tried it in 1984.

12. **True.** Since 1968 you can always find ND games on the radio dial.

13. **False.** Don Criqui and Ralph Guglielmi have done the games.

14. **True.** You must not watch his show if you got this wrong.

Ross Browner was the most decorated ND defensive lineman in the '70s.
(Photo courtesy of University of Notre Dame Sports Information Dept.)

National Awards

Notre Dame's Heisman Award winners are well known. But the Heisman is only one of several national awards given annually. There's the Lombardi Award for outstanding lineman, the Outland Trophy for interior lineman, the Walter Camp Trophy and the Maxwell Award for the player of the year, and the Timmie Award for back of the year. More awards than you may have known . . . and all of them have been won by Notre Dame players.

National Awards Multiple Choice

1. Who was the first Notre Dame player to win the Walter Camp Trophy, given since 1969 to the outstanding individual collegiate player?

    A. Tom Clements
    B. Wayne Bullock
    C. Joe Montana
    D. Ken MacAfee

2. Who is the only Notre Dame player to win both the Lombardi Award for best lineman and the Outland Trophy for best interior lineman?

   A. George Connor
   B. Walt Patulski
   C. George Kunz
   D. Ross Browner

3. Who is the only Notre Dame linebacker to have won the Maxwell Award as the top player in college football?

   A. Bob Crable
   B. Frank Stams
   C. Greg Collins
   D. Jim Lynch

4. Who is the last Notre Dame player to win the Maxwell Award?

   A. Rocket Ismail
   B. Tony Rice
   C. Joe Montana
   D. Ross Browner

5. Which of the following Heisman Award winners did not win the Maxwell Award?

   A. Leon Hart
   B. John Lattner
   C. John Huarte
   D. Tim Brown

6. Who is the only Notre Dame player to win the Maxwell Award twice?

   A. Leon Hart
   B. John Lattner
   C. John Lujack
   D. Angelo Bertelli

7. The most recent Notre Dame player to win the Lombardi Award is:

   A. Tim Ruddy
   B. Aaron Taylor
   C. Chris Zorich
   D. Bryant Young

8. The most recent player to win the Walter Camp Trophy is:

   A. Tim Brown
   B. Tony Rice
   C. Rocket Ismail
   D. Allen Pinkett

9. Three Notre Dame men were inducted into the College Football Hall of Fame in 1951, its inaugural year. Who among the following four was not in that first class of inductees?

   A. Jim Crowley
   B. Elmer Layden
   C. Knute Rockne
   D. George Gipp

10. Only one Heisman-winning back has not won the Timmie Award in the year he also won the Heisman. Who is it?

   A. Tim Brown
   B. John Huarte
   C. Paul Hornung
   D. John Lujack

11. Who was the first Notre Dame player to win the Outland Trophy?

   A. Ziggy Czarobski
   B. Bob Dove
   C. George Connor
   D. Bill Fischer

12. This Notre Dame tight end was inducted into the College Football Hall of Fame in 1997.

   A. Tony Hunter
   B. Dave Casper
   C. Ken MacAfee
   D. Irv Smith

True or False

1. _____ Walt Patulski won the Lombardi Award in 1971.

2. _____ Steve Niehaus won the Outland Trophy in 1975.

3. _____ Emil "Red" Sitko won the Timmie Award in 1949.

4. _____ Quarterback Ralph Guglielmi won the Timmie Award in 1954.

5. _____ Vagas Ferguson won the Timmie Award in 1980.

6. _____ Bob Crable won the Bednarik Award as best linebacker in 1981.

7. _____ Mike Stonebreaker finished third twice in the Butkus Award voting for nation's best linebacker.

8. _____ Rick Mirer won the Davey O'Brien Award as top quarterback in 1992.

9. _____ Derrick Mayes was a semifinalist for the Biletnikoff Award in 1994 and 1995.

10. _____ Todd Lyght won the Thorpe Award as the best defensive back in 1989.

By the Numbers

Match these award winners with their uniform numbers.

1. Ken MacAfee	**A.** 61
2. Ross Browner	**B.** 81
3. Aaron Taylor	**C.** 14
4. Chris Zorich	**D.** 3
5. George Connor	**E.** 72
6. Bill Fischer	**F.** 81
7. Ralph Guglielmi	**G.** 50
8. Emil Sitko	**H.** 81
9. Tim Brown	**I.** 89
10. Jim Lynch	**J.** 73

Multiple Choice
ANSWERS

1. **D:** The big tight end won it in 1977.

2. **D:** Browner won the Outland in 1976 and the Lombardi in 1977. The Outland ruled out Browner in 1977 since he was an end and they were limited to "interior" linemen.

3. **D:** The captain of the 1966 national championship team got some much deserved recognition.

4. **D:** The third of Browner's big awards was this one in 1977.

5. **C & D:** Neither Huarte nor Brown got the nod from the Philadelphia organization that bestows the Maxwell Award.

6. **B:** Lattner won in 1952 and 1953.

7. **B:** Taylor won in 1993, Zorich won in 1990. The others did not win this award.

8. **C:** Rocket won in 1990, Brown in 1987.

9. **A:** Crowley was elected in 1966.

10. **B:** Brown must have qualified as a "flanker back." Huarte did not get this.

11. **C:** Connor won first in 1946. Fischer followed in 1948.

12. **C:** The big man from Brockton, Massachusetts was unstoppable in the 1997 season.

True or False
ANSWERS

1. **True.**

2. **False.**

3. **True.**

4. **True.**

5. **False.**

6. **False.** The award had not yet been created.

7. **True.**

8. **False.**

9. **True.** Like Stonebreaker, he couldn't get over the hump and win it.

10. **False.**

By the Numbers
ANSWERS

1. **B,F,H,** Ken MacAfee, 81

2. **I,** Ross Browner, 89

3. **J,** Aaron Taylor, 73

4. **G,** Chris Zorich, 50

5. **B,F,H,** George Connor, 81

6. **E,** Bill Fischer, 72

7. **D,** Ralph Guglielmi, 3

8. **C,** Emil Sitko, 14

9. **B,F,H,** Tim Brown, 81

10. **A,** Jim Lynch, 61

The defensive line for the 1977 championship team: Fry, Calhoun, Weston, Browner
(Photo courtesy of Willie Fry & the South Bend Tribune*)*

Offensive and Defensive Linemen

How many times has it been said "the game is won in the trenches"? Notre Dame's success can certainly be attributed to many outstanding linemen on both sides of the ball. Here are some tidbits about them.

Player-Number Match

Match the player with their number.

1.	Gerry DiNardo	**A.**	75
2.	Larry DiNardo	**B.**	19
3.	George Connor	**C.**	52
4.	Dick Arrington	**D.**	72
5.	Jack Cannon	**E.**	78
6.	Jerry Groom	**F.**	81
7.	Bill Fischer	**G.**	56
8.	Pat Filley	**H.**	72
9.	Aaron Taylor	**I.**	63
10.	Dave Huffman	**J.**	70
11.	Mike McCoy	**K.**	57
12.	George Kunz	**L.**	50
13.	Greg Marx	**M.**	81
14.	Steve Niehaus	**N.**	56
15.	Walt Patulski	**O.**	71
16.	Alan Page	**P.**	77
17.	John Scully	**Q.**	75
18.	Jim White	**R.**	85

Multiple Choice

1. Which of the following Notre Dame linemen did not finish in the top ten in the Heisman voting?

   A. Ross Browner
   B. Steve Niehaus
   C. Walt Patulski
   D. Mike McCoy

2. Who was the last defensive lineman to lead Notre Dame in tackles?

   A. Wally Kleine
   B. Ross Browner
   C. Bob Golic
   D. Steve Niehaus

3. This defensive lineman was on Pittsburgh's 1996 Super Bowl squad. Who was he?

   A. Bryant Young
   B. Junior Bryant
   C. Oliver Gibson
   D. Paul Grasmanis

4. Which of these players was *not* a member of two national championship squads?

   A. Ross Browner
   B. Willie Fry
   C. George Connor
   D. Ziggy Czarobski

5. Which of these ND players was the first NFL Defensive Player of the Year in 1972?

    A. Mike McCoy
    B. Walt Patulski
    C. Alan Page
    D. Mike Fanning

Matchups

Match the player with the feat.

WHAT?	WHO?
1. This Notre Dame lineman played in four Super Bowls as a member of the Miami Dolphins.	**A.** Andy Heck
2. This tackle played for Atlanta and the Baltimore Colts in the NFL.	**B.** Joe Scibelli
3. This Parseghian-era lineman also played for the Denver Broncos for seven seasons.	**C.** John Scully
4. This tight end blocked for O. J. Simpson as a tackle for the Buffalo Bills.	**D.** Junior Bryant
5. This brother combination played offensive line for the Vikings and the Packers in the NFL.	**E.** Bob and Mike Golic
6. This brother combination played defense for the Browns,	**F.** Dave and Tim Huffman

WHAT?	WHO?
Raiders, Eagles, and Dolphins, among others.	
7. This center snapped the ball to Joe Montana when he played quarterback for the Kansas City Chiefs and through 1996 is still their starting center.	**G.** Bob Dahl
8. This defensive lineman was a #1 pick of the Rams in 1975.	**H.** Tim Grunhard
9. He played defensive line at Notre Dame, but has played offensive line for Cleveland and Washington in the NFL.	**I.** Phil Pozderac
10. He was a fixture offensive guard for the LA Rams from 1961–1975	**J.** Mike Fanning
11. The big tackle played five years in the NFL for the Dallas Cowboys.	**K.** George Kunz
12. An All-American center at Notre Dame, he played nine years for the Atlanta Falcons.	**L.** Bob Kuechenberg
13. A captain of the 1988 national championship team, he was a first-round draft pick of the Seattle Seahawks and is now a starting offensive tackle for the Chicago Bears.	**M.** Paul Costa
14. This Omaha, Nebraska, native has been part of the defensive line rotation of the San Francisco 49ers since 1993.	**N.** Pete Duranko

Player-Number Match
ANSWERS

1. Gerry DiNardo, 72	**10.** Dave Huffman, 56
2. Larry DiNardo, 56	**11.** Mike McCoy, 77
3. George Connor, 81	**12.** George Kunz, 78
4. Dick Arrington, 63	**13.** Greg Marx, 75
5. Jack Cannon, 19	**14.** Steve Niehaus, 70
6. Jerry Groom, 50	**15.** Walt Patulski, 85
7. Bill Fischer, 72	**16.** Alan Page, 81
8. Pat Filley, 52	**17.** John Scully, 57
9. Aaron Taylor, 75	**18.** Jim White, 71

Multiple Choice
ANSWERS

1. B: Niehaus finished 12th in 1975.

2. D: Niehaus had 113 tackles in 1977.

3. C: Maybe this was Gibson's reward for suffering through the difficult 1995 season.

4. D: Czarobski was on three national championship teams at ND 1943, '46, and '47.

5. C: Page was the ringleader of the "Purple People Eaters" in Minnesota.

Matchup

ANSWERS

1. **L**, Bob Kuechenberg	8. **J**, Mike Fanning
2. **K**, George Kunz	9. **G**, Bob Dahl
3. **N**, Pete Duranko	10. **B**, Joe Scibelli
4. **M**, Paul Costa	11. **I**, Phil Pozderac
5. **F**, Dave and Tim Huffman	12. **C**, John Scully
6. **E**, Bob and Mike Golic	13. **A**, Andy Heck
7. **H**, Tim Grunhard	14. **D**, Junior Bryant

Parseghian revived the Notre Dame football program in the mid-sixties.
(Photo courtesy of University of Notre Dame Sports Information Dept.)

Parseghian

The era of Ara was a period when Notre Dame emerged from a decade of down seasons that followed the successes of Frank Leahy. Notre Dame was very familiar with Parseghian because he had been a difficult nemesis while at Northwestern. Ara arrived on campus in 1964 and like Lou Holtz, who followed 22 seasons later, he immediately made Notre Dame a winner again.

Parseghian Picks

1. Which Notre Dame coach preceded Ara?

   A. Joe Kuharich
   B. Hugh Devore
   C. Terry Brennan
   D. Dan Devine

2. Whom was Devore forced into service to replace?

   A. Terry Brennan
   B. Elmer Layden
   C. Joe Kuharich
   D. Myran Pottios

3. What was Ara's record in his first season?

   A. 10–0
   B. 8–2
   C. 9–1
   D. 8–1–1

4. Who was that sole loss to in '64?

   A. Michigan State
   B. Northwestern
   C. Navy
   D. USC

5. Parseghian's teams featured many great passing combinations. Which one produced the most yards in a season?

   A. John Huarte to Jack Snow
   B. Terry Hanratty to Jim Seymour

   C. Joe Theismann to Tom Gatewood
   D. Tom Clements to Pete Demmerle

6. Which of those combinations scored the most touchdowns in a season?

   A. John Huarte to Jack Snow
   B. Terry Hanratty to Jim Seymour
   C. Joe Theismann to Tom Gatewood
   D. Tom Clements to Pete Demmerle

7. How many times did Notre Dame finish in the AP top ten during Parseghian's first seven years?

   A. Five
   B. Six
   C. Seven
   D. Four

8. What was Ara's record against Notre Dame while he coached at Northwestern?

   A. 3–1
   B. 2–2
   C. 3–2
   D. 4–0

9. Parseghian started his coaching career as an assistant at Miami of Ohio. Who was the head coach there at that time?

   A. Paul Brown
   B. Bo Schembechler
   C. Woody Hayes
   D. Lee Corso

10. What pro team did Parseghian play for?

    A. Chicago Bears
    B. Detroit Lions
    C. Cincinnati Bengals
    D. Cleveland Browns

11. What was Ara's record against USC while he was at the Notre Dame helm?

    A. 4–7
    B. 4–6–1
    C. 3–6–2
    D. 5–6

12. He is the only Notre Dame running back to rank in the top 20 in career yardage who played exclusively for Ara.

    A. Nick Eddy
    B. Larry Conjar
    C. Wayne Bullock
    D. Al Hunter

13. Which of these players who won a national championship under Parseghian did not win a Super Bowl as well?

    A. Joe Theismann
    B. Dave Casper
    C. Alan Page
    D. Bob Kuechenberg

14. Which Parseghian-era assistant coach was part of the three-member team that recommended Bob Davie to succeed Lou Holtz as head coach?

    A. Brian Boulac
    B. Joe Yonto

C. Tom Pagna
D. George Kelly

15. Two brothers with this last name were both consensus All-Americans under Ara:

A. Demmerle
B. Allocco
C. DiNardo
D. Browner

16. Which two brothers were teammates on the 1973 national championship team?

A. Browner
B. Allocco
C. DiNardo
D. Townsend

Ara's Pairings

WHAT?	WHO?
1. He was Ara's offensive coordinator.	**A.** Joe Theismann
2. He was on Parseghian's staff and still broadcasts Notre Dame's games on radio.	**B.** Jack Snow
3. He was the captain of Ara's first national championship team in 1966.	**C.** John Huarte

WHAT?	WHO?
4. This Parseghian quarterback still holds the record for most rushing yards in a game by a Notre Dame quarterback.	**D.** Ross Browner
5. This Parseghian quarterback holds the record for most passing yards in a game with 512.	**E.** Mike Townsend
6. This freshman defensive lineman sacked Gary Rutledge in the 1973 Sugar Bowl to end a 4th-quarter Alabama drive and help preserve the victory.	**F.** Jim Carroll
7. This halfback on Notre Dame's 1963 team became the "go-to" receiver in 1964.	**G.** Tom Pagna
8. A third-string quarterback in 1963, he won the Heisman Trophy in 1964.	**H.** Bob Gladieux
9. He scored the first points of the 1973 national championship season.	**I.** Joe Montana
10. This player served as Ara's first captain.	**J.** Gerry DiNardo
11. This defensive back played for Ara and Digger Phelps in the same season.	**K.** Tom Pagna
12. This quarterback was originally recruited by Ara but never played a down for him.	**L.** Jim Lynch

WHAT?	WHO?
13. He's the highest ranking seasonal scoring leader from Parseghian's tenure.	**M.** Bill Etter
14. This Parseghian All-American went on to be head coach at Vanderbilt and LSU.	**N.** Ross Browner

True or False

1. _____ Ara was the first non-Catholic to be head coach at Notre Dame.

2. _____ Parseghian, Leahy, and Holtz all coached the same number of seasons at Notre Dame.

3. _____ A Notre Dame defensive back led the country in interceptions twice during Parseghian's tenure.

4. _____ Despite his great teams, Parseghian never had a player drafted #1 overall.

5. _____ Notre Dame's consecutive sellout streak began under Parseghian.

6. _____ No Parseghian back ever rushed for 1,000 yards.

7. _____ No Parseghian kicker ever went on to success in the professional ranks.

8. _____ Parseghian lost only one game to Purdue in his tenure.

Parseghian Picks
ANSWERS

1. **B:** For the second time Devore jumped in to coach the Irish for a single season. He had previously stepped in for Frank Leahy when Leahy was called to active duty in World War II.

2. **C:** In February of 1963 Kuharich resigned to become supervisor of officials for the National Football League. Since that timing made it difficult to find a worthy successor, Father Joyce asked Hugh Devore to step in on an interim basis.

3. **C:** There was only one blemish on the record.

4. **D:** Yep, those damn Trojans spoiled a possible national championship with a 20–17 victory at Notre Dame's very own House of Pain, the LA Coliseum.

5. **C:** Theismann to Gatewood totaled 1,123 yards in 1970 on 77 receptions.

6. **A:** Huarte to Snow as good for nine touchdowns in 1964. Hanratty to Seymour was good for eight in '66.

7. **D:** It's almost hard to believe, but Ara immediately made the Irish a fixture at the top of college football.

8. **D:** If you can't beat him, hire him!

9. **C:** Although all of those coaches worked at the "cradle of coaches," Hayes was the head coach when Parseghian started.

10. **D:** Ara was there before the Pound and before Modell.

11. **C:** If only he could have mastered the Trojans he might have won four national titles.

12. **C:** Don't forget that Hunter also played for Dan Devine!

13. **C:** All of them got there at least once, but Alan Page never won it as he played for the perpetual bridesmaids of the 70s: The Minnesota Vikings.

14. **D:** George Kelly was an assistant coach for Dan Devine and Gerry Faust as well before he joined the ND Athletic Administration. With Father Beauchamp and Mike Wadsworth, he conducted the coaching search.

15. **C:** Larry and Gerry from New York City both were consensus All-Americans under Parseghian.

16. **D:** Mike was a star defensive back and Willie a wide receiver.

Ara's Pairings
ANSWERS

1. **G, K,** Tom Pagna

2. **G, K,** Tom Pagna

3. **L,** Jim Lynch

4. **M,** Bill Etter

5. **A,** Joe Theismann

6. **D, N,** Ross Browner

7. **B,** Jack Snow

8. **C,** John Huarte

9. **D, N,** Ross Browner

10. **F,** Jim Carroll

11. **E,** Mike Townsend

12. **I,** Joe Montana

13. **H,** Bob Gladieux

14. **J,** Gerry DiNardo

True or False
ANSWERS

1. **True.**

2. **True.**

3. **True.** Tony Carey in 1964 and Mike Townsend in 1972

4. **False.** Walt Patulski by Buffalo in 1972

5. **True.** After the Thanksgiving weekend Air Force non-sellout in 1972

6. **True.** Wayne Bullock was closest with 855 yards in 1974.

7. **False.** Remember Bob Thomas

8. **False.** Purdue was a major nemesis for Ara. His teams went 6–5 versus the Boilermakers.

Quarterbacks

Other schools have their positions, but quarterback is *the one* at Notre Dame. Penn State makes linebackers, USC is tailback U, but Notre Dame is a quarterback kind of place. With such a rich quarterback history and many interesting stories there's plenty of trivia. Enjoy.

Multiple Choice

1. Who was the last Notre Dame quarterback to become a consensus All-American?

   A. Terry Hanratty
   B. Joe Theismann
   C. Joe Montana
   D. Tom Clements

2. Which quarterback was the first to complete more than 100 passes in a season for Notre Dame?

   A. Paul Hornung
   B. John Huarte
   C. Terry Hanratty
   D. Bob Williams

3. How many touchdown passes did Daryle Lamonica, later known as the "Mad Bomber" with the Oakland Raiders, throw when he was the starting quarterback in 1962?

   A. Zero
   B. Two
   C. Four
   D. Six

4. Who has more career completions at Notre Dame, Joe Theismann or Blair Kiel?

   A. Theismann
   B. Kiel

5. Which of the following quarterbacks *did not* throw more career touchdowns than Joe Montana?

   A. Ron Powlus
   B. Terry Hanratty
   C. Tom Clements
   D. Steve Beuerlein

6. Who started the 1987 season, Holtz's second at Notre Dame, at quarterback?

   A. Tony Rice
   B. Kent Graham
   C. Terry Andrysiak
   D. Pete Graham

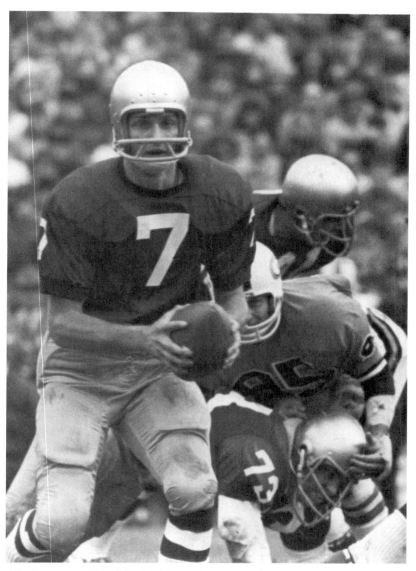
Theismann still holds the Notre Dame single-game passing record.
(Photo courtesy of University of Notre Dame Sports Information Dept.)

7. Which of the following Notre Dame quarterbacks did not hail from Pennsylvania?

    A. Tom Clements
    B. Ron Powlus
    C. Joe Montana
    D. Joe Theismann

8. Only one of the following quarterbacks was also a team captain at Notre Dame. Who was it?

    A. Joe Theismann
    B. Steve Beuerlein
    C. John Huarte
    D. Joe Montana

9. Which quarterback holds the record for highest completion percentage in a season?

    A. Joe Theismann
    B. Steve Beuerlein
    C. Tom Clements
    D. Kevin McDougal

10. Which quarterback holds the career record for completion percentage?

    A. Joe Theismann
    B. Steve Beuerlein
    C. Tom Clements
    D. Joe Montana

11. Which quarterback is the career total offense leader?

    A. Joe Theismann
    B. Steve Beuerlein
    C. Rick Mirer
    D. Tony Rice

12. Which of the following quarterbacks has also been an assistant coach for the Irish?

  A. Terry Hanratty
  B. Paul Hornung
  C. Tom Clements
  D. Tony Rice

13. Which of the following Irish quarterbacks did not hail from California?

  A. John Huarte
  B. Steve Beuerlein
  C. Daryle Lamonica
  D. Tom Krug
  E. Kevin Muno
  F. Rich Slager

14. Who was the last Notre Dame quarterback to lead the team in passing with less than 1,000 yards?

  A. Blair Kiel
  B. Terry Andrysiak
  C. Tony Rice
  D. Kevin McDougal

15. George Gipp wore which of the following numbers?

  A. 1
  B. 2
  C. 3
  D. 5
  E. None

Match the Description with the Appropriate Player

WHAT?	WHO?
1. He was Knute's quarterback, the one who threw him passes when Rockne played for the Irish.	**A.** Daryle Lamonica
2. He was Holtz's first quarterback and he went on to a successful NFL career.	**B.** Tom Krug
3. This option quarterback piloted Holtz's only national championship team.	**C.** Terry Andrysiak
4. This quarterback started ahead of Joe Montana in the 1977 national championship season.	**D.** Tim Koegel
5. He was the quarterback on the "almost" national title team in 1993, maybe just because Ron Powlus was injured.	**E.** Ron Powlus
6. He was a starting quarterback for Dan Devine in 1980 and Gerry Faust in 1981 and 1982.	**F.** Steve Beuerlein
7. He was the quarterback between Huarte and Hanratty.	**G.** Gus Dorais
8. He started the 1971 season as the quarterback between Theismann and Clements.	**H.** Tony Rice

WHAT?	WHO?
9. He finished the 1971 season as quarterback and later in his career backed up Clements.	**I.** Rusty Lisch
10. He holds the record for touchdown passes in a career at Notre Dame.	**J.** Kevin McDougal
11. This product of Cincinnati's Moeller High later played for his high school coach at Notre Dame.	**K.** Blair Kiel
12. This quarterback started the 1988 Cotton Bowl, Lou Holtz's first bowl game at Notre Dame.	**L.** Bill Zloch
13. He filled in for an injured Ron Powlus in 1995 and led the Irish into the Orange Bowl.	**M.** Bill Etter
14. He quarterbacked the '60–'62 Irish teams and later led the Oakland Raiders to an AFL title.	**N.** Cliff Brown

By the Numbers

Certain numbers, especially single digits, have been used again and again by Notre Dame quarterbacks. Match the following quarterbacks with the number they wore.

1. Ron Powlus	**A.** 5
2. Steve Beuerlein	**B.** 9
3. Joe Montana	**C.** 5
4. Tom Clements	**D.** 7
5. Paul Hornung	**E.** 15
6. Terry Hanratty	**F.** 9
7. Joe Theismann	**G.** 3
8. Blair Kiel	**H.** 48
9. Rick Mirer	**I.** 14
10. Tony Rice	**J.** 6
11. Kevin McDougal	**K.** 32
12. Bob Williams	**L.** 7
13. John Lujack	**M.** 7
14. Angelo Bertelli	**N.** 3
15. John Lattner	**O.** 5
16. John Huarte	**P.** 3
17. Rusty Lisch	**Q.** 2

True or False

1. _____ The first Notre Dame quarterback selected in the first round of the NFL draft was Angelo Bertelli.

2. _____ In 1946 two Notre Dame quarterbacks were selected in the first round of the NFL draft.

3. _____ No Notre Dame quarterback was drafted by the NFL in the first round from 1960 until Rick Mirer went #2 overall in 1993.

4. _____ George Gipp led the Irish in passing in 1918, 1919, and 1920.

5. _____ John Huarte had thrown only 20 passes for Notre Dame before he took the quarterback's reins in 1964.

6. _____ Jim Crowley was the quarterback in the Four Horsemen backfield of 1924.

7. _____ Through the 1996 season the last Notre Dame quarterback to be on the roster of a Super Bowl team was Joe Montana.

8. _____ Although he was on the Pittsburgh Steelers, Terry Hanratty was never active for a Super Bowl game.

9. _____ Joe Montana doesn't even rank in the top five for total offense in his career at Notre Dame.

10. _____ Only Steve Beuerlein is over 6,000 yards in career passing at Notre Dame.

Multiple Choice
ANSWERS

1. **A:** Hard to believe but true.

2. **B:** Williams came closest with 99 in 1950 until Huarte topped it.

3. **D:** The quality of the team may have had something to do with that low number as the '62 squad went 5–5.

4. **B:** Theismann threw for more yardage but Kiel had seven more completions.

5. **C:** Montana had 25 career touchdowns, Clements had 24.

6. **C:** Andrysiak was hurt in the fourth game of 1987 and Tony Rice took over.

7. **D:** Theismann is a Jersey guy, South River to be exact.

8. **D:** Montana was captain of the 1978 squad.

9. **D:** Beuerlein was the first to be over 60% for a season in 1984 with a .603, but Kevin McDougal topped that with .616 in 1993.

10. **A:** Through 1996 Theismann is tops with .569, but Powlus may challenge that as he returns in 1997.

11. **C:** Through 1996, it's Mirer, but Powlus can threaten this as well.

12. **C:** Clements was an assistant coach under Holtz in the 90s.

13. **E:** Who says the Irish can't recruit California. Look at all those California-produced quarterbacks. Slager, by the way, is from Columbus, OH.

14. **C:** Rice stepped in after Andrysiak was injured in 1987 and finished with 663 yards passing.

15. **E:** There were no numbers in Gipp's day.

Match the Description
ANSWERS

1. **G,** Gus Dorais

2. **F,** Steve Beuerlein

3. **H,** Tony Rice

4. **I,** Rusty Lisch

5. **J,** Kevin McDougal

6. **K,** Blair Kiel

7. **L,** Bill Zloch

8. **M,** Bill Etter

9. **N,** Cliff Brown

10. **E,** Ron Powlus

11. **D,** Tim Koegel

12. **C,** Terry Andrysiak

13. **B,** Tom Krug

14. **A,** Daryle Lamonica

Quarterback Numbers
ANSWERS

1. Ron Powlus, 3

2. Steve Beuerlein, 7

3. Joe Montana, 3

4. Tom Clements, 2

5. Paul Hornung, 5

6. Terry Hanratty, 5

7. Joe Theismann, 7	13. John Lujack, 32
8. Blair Kiel, 5	14. Angelo Bertelli, 48
9. Rick Mirer, 3	15. John Lattner, 14
10. Tony Rice, 9	16. John Huarte, 7
11. Kevin McDougal, 15	17. Rusty Lisch, 6
12. Bob Williams, 9	

True or False
ANSWERS

1. **True.**

2. **True.** Both Johnny Lujack and Frank Dancewicz went in the first round.

3. **True.** Lamonica, Huarte, Hanratty, Theismann, Clements, Montana, Beuerlein, and Rice all were unworthy of #1 status according to NFL talent gurus.

4. **True.** The legend had incredible statistics for his day.

5. **False.** Huarte had attempted 50 passes total in the 1962 and '63 seasons.

6. **False.** Harry Stuhldreher was quarterback. Crowley was the left halfback.

7. **False.** Steve Beuerlein was on the 1993 Dallas Cowboys Super Bowl team.

8. **False.** Hanratty was inactive in 1975 for the Steelers' first Super Bowl versus Minnesota but was active in 1976 versus Dallas.

9. **True.** He split time with Rick Slager early in his career and Rusty Lisch later.

10. **True.** When you're behind you have to pass more.

Rockne has the highest winning percentage in NCAA history.
(Photo courtesy of University of Notre Dame Sports Information Dept.)

Rockne

Knute Rockne. The man who started it all. Or, at the very least, the man who started to make it famous. Rockne played for Notre Dame and coached the team during its rise to national prominence. He had a gift for publicity as well as being a great teacher and motivator. His tragic death was mourned throughout the country.

Multiple Choice

1. How many seasons did Notre Dame field a team before Rockne appeared on the roster?

    A. 10
    B. 15
    C. 17
    D. 22

2. What position did Rockne play?

    A. Right halfback
    B. Left halfback
    C. Quarterback
    D. Left end

3. Rockne earned his first monogram in what sport?

   A. Baseball
   B. Track and field
   C. Boxing
   D. Tennis

4. In what track-and-field event did Rockne set a school record?

   A. 100-yard dash
   B. Shot put
   C. Pole vault
   D. 60-meter hurdles

5. In addition to track and field, Rockne did many things during his student days. Which of the following didn't he do?

   A. Write for the student newspaper
   B. Write for the yearbook
   C. Reach the finals of a marbles tournament
   D. Play flute in the school orchestra
   E. Box semiprofessionally
   F. None of the above

6. Rockne started coaching under Jess Harper while he was a graduate assistant in this subject.

   A. History
   B. Biology
   C. Chemistry
   D. Economics

7. Rockne's family moved from Norway to what U.S. city?

   A. South Bend
   B. Cincinnati
   C. Kansas City
   D. Chicago

8. What was the only bowl game Rockne coached in?

   A. Orange Bowl
   B. Sugar Bowl
   C. Cotton Bowl
   D. Rose Bowl

9. What offensive formation did Rockne become famous for?

   A. Single wing
   B. Shotgun
   C. Notre Dame shift
   D. Wishbone

10. What Notre Dame figure later bought Rockne's summer house on the shores of Lake Michigan?

   A. Moose Krause
   B. Paul Hornung
   C. Digger Phelps
   D. Lou Holtz

True or False

1. _____ Rockne has the highest winning percentage as a coach in NCAA history at .881.

2. _____ Rockne won a national title in the last season he coached, 1930.

3. _____ Rockne considered leaving Notre Dame for USC.

4. _____ Gus Dorais, Rockne's quarterback, was the first Notre Dame player to win first-team All-American status on any team.

5. _____ Rockne was a first-team All-American according to Walter Camp.

6. _____ Ernie Nevers was the star of the Stanford team Notre Dame defeated in the 1925 Rose Bowl.

7. _____ Rockne's team had won 19 straight games at the time of his death.

8. _____ The last team to beat Rockne was USC in 1928.

9. _____ Each of the five times Notre Dame played at Soldier field in Chicago under Rockne they played to more than 100,000 fans.

10. _____ Rockne caught a then-record pass of 40 yards against Army in 1913.

11. _____ Rockne coached only one season in the stadium he designed: Notre Dame Stadium.

12. _____ Rockne was traveling to shoot an instructional video when his plane crashed near Bazaar, Kansas.

13. _____ Rockne was the first undergraduate to serve as a student instructor while at Notre Dame.

14. _____ Notre Dame was undefeated when Rockne was on the varsity.

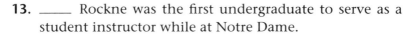

Multiple Choice
ANSWERS

1. **D:** Rockne played from 1911–13; Notre Dame first played in 1888.

2. **D:** Rockne was starting LE for three seasons.

3. **B:** Rockne was a track man.

4. **C:** Rockne cleared 12–4 in the indoor vault.

5. **F:** He was a true Renaissance man.

6. **C:** He assisted Professor Julius Nieuwland, who discovered synthetic rubber.

7. **D:** The best thing Chicago ever did was send him to Notre Dame.

8. **D:** Notre Dame won the 1925 game that featured the Four Horsemen.

9. **C:** The Notre Dame shift put all four backs in motion prior to the snaps. This so confused opponents that it was eventually outlawed.

10. **C:** Too bad some of the Rock's magic didn't rub off on him.

True or False
ANSWERS

1. **True.**

2. **True.**

3. **True.** According to the best information available

4. **True.**

5. **False.** He was a third-team selection.

6. **True.** Rockne never ducked a tough opponent.

7. **True.**

8. **True.** The Trojans won 27–14 in Los Angeles.

9. **False.** Four out of five times they did have over 100,000. Once against Drake, they only drew 50,000.

10. **True.**

11. **True.**

12. **True.**

13. **True.**

14. **True.** Notre Dame was 20–0–2 in Rockne's three years as a player.

Seven Stars: The Heisman Award Winners

There was a time when the phrase "Notre Dame Heisman Trophy winner" seemed almost redundant. Over a fourteen-season period in the forties and fifties, five Notre Dame players won the coveted award. It's been a while, but Notre Dame players are always mentioned as possible candidates.

Heisman Multiple Choice

1. Which Notre Dame player did not finish second in the Heisman voting?
   - **A.** Joe Theismann
   - **B.** Rocket Ismail
   - **C.** Terry Hanratty
   - **D.** Angelo Bertelli

2. Which Heisman Trophy winner did not play in the NFL?
   - **A.** Angelo Bertelli
   - **B.** Johnny Lujack
   - **C.** John Huarte
   - **D.** Leon Hart

John Lujack,
Quarterback, 1947

Angelo Bertelli, Quarterback, 1943

Leon Hart, Right
End, 1949

John Lattner,
Halfback, 1953

3. Tim Brown's two punt returns for touchdowns against this team put him in the early lead for the 1987 Heisman award.

A. Michigan

B. Michigan State

C. Purdue

D. Navy

Paul Hornung, Quarterback, 1956

John Huarte, Quarterback, 1964
(Photos courtesy of University of Notre Dame Sports Information Dept.)

Tim Brown, Flanker, 1987
(Photo by Steve Navratil)

4. Who is the only Heisman Trophy winner to play for a losing team?

   A. Johnny Lattner
   B. Paul Hornung
   C. Tim Brown
   D. Leon Hart

5. Which Notre Dame Heisman winner wasn't even a starter the year before he won the award?

   A. Tim Brown
   B. Angelo Bertelli
   C. Johnny Lattner
   D. John Huarte

6. Which Notre Dame Heisman winner did not even complete the fall season in which he won the honor?

   A. Paul Hornung
   B. Johnny Lattner
   C. Johnny Lujack
   D. Angelo Bertelli

7. Which eventual Heisman Trophy winner fumbled the very first time he touched the ball in a game situation?

   A. Paul Hornung
   B. John Lujack
   C. John Huarte
   D. Tim Brown

8. This eventual Heisman winner jumped to the head of the pack with a great early-season performance against Notre Dame.

   A. Herschel Walker

B. Rashaan Salaam
C. Desmond Howard
D. Ty Detmer

9. Which Heisman winner went on to win an NFL championship and a Super Bowl?

A. John Huarte
B. Leon Hart
C. Johnny Lujack
D. Paul Hornung

10. Which Heisman winner was a teammate of Joe Namath's?

A. John Huarte
B. Leon Hart
C. Johnny Lujack
D. Paul Hornung

11. Which Heisman Trophy winner led Notre Dame in no offensive categories the year he was selected?

A. Johnny Lujack
B. Johnny Lattner
C. John Huarte
D. Leon Hart

12. Whose Heisman Trophy might have gone to a Notre Dame player if the voting happened after all the games he played?

A. Eddie George
B. Gino Toretta
C. Rashaan Salaam
D. Ty Detmer

Heisman Matchups

MATCHUP	WHO?
1. This Notre Dame player said he would have won the Heisman if he had been kept at running back.	**A.** John Huarte
2. The Golden Boy.	**B.** Herschel Walker
3. The Springfield Rifle.	**C.** Terry Hanratty
4. Played for the same high school as Steve Beuerlein.	**D.** Ricky Watters
5. Finished in the top ten in Heisman voting three times but never won it.	**E.** Angelo Bertelli
6. All-time leading receiver for Notre Dame but was never considered by Heisman voters.	**F.** Eddie George
7. Heisman winner who was shut down by Notre Dame in the 1978 Cotton Bowl.	**G.** Doug Flutie
8. First nonback to win the Heisman.	**H.** Leon Hart
9. Second nonback to win the Heisman.	**I.** Rashaan Salaam
10. Beaten by Notre Dame in the 1983 Liberty Bowl.	**J.** Earl Campbell
11. Beat Notre Dame with his powerful running in the 1980 Sugar Bowl.	**K.** Paul Hornung

MATCHUP	WHO?
12. Ran all over Notre Dame in the 1995 Fiesta Bowl.	**L.** Tom Gatewood
13. Ran almost at will against Notre Dame during their meeting in the 1996 season.	**M.** Tim Brown

Heisman True or False

1. ____ The only non-quarterback or running back winners of the Heisman Trophy are Notre Dame players: Leon Hart and Tim Brown.

2. ____ Even though he tormented the Irish, especially in 1974, USC running back Anthony Davis never won the Heisman Trophy.

3. ____ The Heisman award was originally going to be named the Rockne award in memory of the legendary coach.

4. ____ Tim Brown's Heisman win may have cost Rocket Ismail the trophy in 1990.

5. ____ Leon Hart was the only Heisman winner to play on both sides of the ball.

6. ____ Nick Eddy, a featured running back in the mid-sixties, never generated many Heisman votes.

7. ____ Joe Montana was the highest Notre Dame vote getter in the 1977 Heisman race.

8. ____ Allen Pinkett never cracked the top ten in Heisman voting because he played on some poor, by Notre Dame standards, teams.

9. _____ No Notre Dame player has won the Heisman when other teammates have finished in the top ten of the voting.

10. _____ Joe Theismann, who had the pronunciation of his last name changed to rhyme with Heisman, lost the 1970 Heisman to Archie Manning.

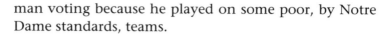

Heisman Multiple Choice
ANSWERS

1. **C:** Hanratty's highest finish was third. Bertelli did win the award in 1943 but finished second in 1941.

2. **A:** Bertelli played briefly in the All-American Football Conference, which later merged with the NFL.

3. **B:** The fact that there was a national television audience watching the Irish-Spartans tilt on ESPN didn't hurt matters either.

4. **B:** Hornung won in '56 when the Irish went 2–9. Talk about the power of Notre Dame! Today it would be unlikely for a Heisman winner to come from a non-championship-caliber team.

5. **C:** Huarte owes his success to Ara Parseghian, who rescued him from relative obscurity and put him in the national spotlight.

6. **D:** Bertelli was called into the armed services due to World War II.

7. **D:** Tim Brown fumbled the opening kickoff against Purdue at the Hoosier Dome as a freshman. His career proceeded significantly better after that tough start.

8. **C:** Howard's fourth-down touchdown catch not only sealed the victory but was arguably the most memorable play of the 1991 season. The usually conservative Gary Moeller not only went for it, he called a high-risk fade route that Howard had to fully lay out to catch.

9. **D:** The Packers were as bad as his '56 Irish team when Hornung joined them, but Vince Lombardi quickly turned that situation around.

10. **A:** Huarte was Namath's backup on the Jets in the mid-sixties.

11. **B:** Lattner was the jack-of-all-trades for the Irish. He ran, passed, and gained his way to the Heisman.

12. **D:** Detmer had an interception-filled game the night he won the award in 1990.

Heisman Matchup
ANSWERS

1. **D**, Ricky Watters	8. **H**, Leon Hart
2. **K**, Paul Hornung	9. **M**, Tim Brown
3. **E**, Angelo Bertelli	10. **G**, Doug Flutie
4. **A**, John Huarte	11. **B**, Herschel Walker
5. **C**, Terry Hanratty	12. **I**, Rashaan Salaam
6. **L**, Tom Gatewood	13. **F**, Eddie George
7. **J**, Earl Campbell	

Heisman True or False
ANSWERS

1. **False.** That was true until Michigan's Desmond Howard, a receiver, won the award in 1991.

2. **True.** Although he was a contender and a damaging opponent, he never won.

3. **False.** The award was originally called the D.A.C. award, a reference to the Downtown Athletic Club, which bestows it to this day. Heisman, a former coach, became the D.A.C. athletic director and the award was subsequently named for him.

4. **True.** Some media folks thought the "Notre Dame machine" pushed Brown too hard and that Syracuse's Don McPherson should have won. Come to think of it Syracuse has a pretty good media machine itself.

5. **False.** The forties were the era of one-platoon football and the era of Notre Dame's Heisman Run.

6. **False.** Eddy finished in the top ten in the Heisman balloting twice.

7. **False.** Ken MacAfee and Ross Browner both finished in the top five, while Montana's name didn't show up.

8. **False.** Pinkett finished eighth in 1985 despite a 5–6 season with Gerry Faust at the helm.

9. **False.** Bertelli and Hart each had two teammates in the top ten. Bertelli had Creighton Miller and Jim White in '43. Hart had Bob Williams and Emil "Red" Sitko in '49. So much for the splitting votes theory.

10. **False.** Theismann lost to Stanford's Jim Plunkett. Manning was third in the balloting.

Did you know George Gipp came to Notre Dame to play baseball, not football?
(Photo courtesy of University of Notre Dame Sports Information Dept.)

Transfers, Early Departures, and Late Arrivals

Everybody wants to play for Notre Dame. But that romantic notion can fade when the reality is you are #4 on the coaches' depth chart and all the players in front of you are your age or younger.

The traditional depth of talent has led some interesting players to leave the shadow of the Golden Dome. So too has the call of riches for turning pro. A select few other players have played somewhere else or even played another sport in college before coming to Notre Dame football. Others really wanted to come but never got the chance. See if you can match the player with his situation.

Name the Player

1. This fullback had junior college experience before joining the ND squad during the Faust era. His brother Kerry played quarterback for the Irish in the 70s. _____

2. This Berwick, PA, quarterback preceded Ron Powlus to ND before transferring to West Virginia. _____

3. This fullback, a member of a favorite ND football family, transferred to Tulane after starring for the Devine-era Irish. _____

4. This Parseghian-era halfback transferred to Kent State to complete his collegiate eligibility. _____

5. This Holtz-era lineman transferred to Michigan State after starting for ND. _____

6. This Illinois high school quarterback sat behind Tony Rice before transferring to Ohio State. He then went on to play professional football. _____

7. This Colorado high school tackle wanted to attend Notre Dame in the worst way. He went on to USC and then became an NFL all-pro. _____

8. This receiver/defensive back played at Yale before transferring to ND and walking on to the team. He later played professional football for the Bears and Redskins, among others. _____

9. This Holtz-era quarterback transferred to Virginia. _____

10. This much celebrated wide receiver was denied admission after a high school fight. He went on to star for Marshall University. _____

11. A California quarterback, he played wide receiver, quarterback, and kick returner before transferring to Arizona. _____

12. He matriculated at ND but left for Hollywood. He didn't play football but he knows his "cheers." _____

13. This linebacker was a big factor in the 31–30 upset of Miami in 1988. He later transferred to UCLA. _____

14. This Faust-era quarterback recruit didn't transfer to another school. He went to another sport: baseball. _____

15. This tight end did the same thing, switch to baseball, after he was part of the 1988 national championship team. _____

16. This ND baseball player added football to his activities as a kick returner and wide receiver. He eventually switched back to baseball after signing with the Detroit Tigers. _____

17. This Arizona wide receiver, with the same last name as an ND Heisman Trophy winner, played two years for the Irish before transferring. _____

18. This younger brother of two ND All-Americans left the program and made numerous allegations against Lou Holtz in a *Sports Illustrated* article. _____

19. This *USA Today*–decorated lineman from Chicago also made allegations against Holtz after he left the program. _____

20. This California linebacker returned to his native state to play for the Cal Bears after two noteworthy seasons in South Bend. _____

21. This kicker, the son of an ND alumnus, reneged on a verbal commitment to Holtz and went to Florida State, where he won a national title as a freshman. _____

22. This Irish cornerback left early and was drafted by the Philadelphia Eagles in the second-round 1995 NFL draft. _____

23. "The Bus" left South Bend early after a record-setting Sugar Bowl performance. _____

24. This speed merchant raced to Canada and CFL money after his junior year. _____

25. This running back had one more year left when he entered the NFL supplemental draft. A campus rules violation was alleged. _____

26. He originally committed to Vanderbilt, but this punter switched to ND. He stayed two years before transferring. _____

27. He was originally an Irish soccer player who later pulled double duty by kicking for the 1993 almost championship team. _____

28. This running back was said to be in Notre Dame's sights in the fall of 1995. He later signed with Nebraska. _____

29. He left Notre Dame's secondary after his junior year and was selected in the first round by the Washington Redskins. _____

30. He came to Notre Dame to play lacrosse. He left to play offensive line in the NFL. _____

31. This nose tackle stayed four years in South Bend but could have returned for a fifth since he did not see action during his freshman season. _____

Name the Player
ANSWERS

1. Larry Moriarty

2. Jake Kelchner

3. Willard Browner

4. Art Best

5. Jeff Pearson

6. Kent Graham

7. Tony Boselli

8. Pat Eilers

9. B. J. Hawkins

10. Randy Moss

11. Leon Blunt

12. George Wendt

13. Arnold Ale

14. Pat Pesavento

15. Frank Jacobs

16. Scott Sollmann

17. Speedy Hart

18. Steve Huffman

19. Chet Lacheta

20. John McLaughlin

21. Scott Bentley

22. Bobby Taylor

23. Jerome Bettis

24. Rocket Ismail

25. Al Hunter

26. Brian Ford

27. Kevin Pendergast

28. D'Angelo Evans

29. Tom Carter

30. Mike Brennan

31. Chris Zorich

ND got the best of USC in October of 1973 despite Sam "Bam" Cunningham's efforts.
(Photo courtesy of Tony Pace)

USC

It is the longest running intersectional rivalry in college football . . . a phrase that this series has made famous with every broadcast and promotional message. It started with two legendary coaches, Knute Rockne and Howard Jones. It has had some of the most legendary players in the history of the game . . . from Lujack to Montana for the Irish and Simpson to Allen for the Trojans. Notre Dame versus USC is a game that annually influences the national title. No rivalry has seen more Heisman Trophy winners. It has had some memorable streaks of dominance by both teams. Here are some things you may not have known about Notre Dame vs. USC.

How It Began

Knute Rockne was not only a master tactician and coach; he knew how to promote his team and himself. After the Notre Dame Rose Bowl appearance against Stanford in 1924, the Notre Dame administration decreed a moratorium on bowl games, one that lasted until in 1970 and the Cotton Bowl experience against Texas. Rockne viewed the alternating-year trip to California as a substitute for a bowl game. He also knew that exposure in the West would help his Irish become a truly national team.

The Games for the Ages

There are almost too many memorable games in this series to attempt to highlight just a few, but five games stand out.

1. "That Damn Song"

The most infamous, at least from Irish fans' point of view, was the 1974 55–24 debacle at the Los Angeles Coliseum. Notre Dame had won the previous season in South Bend, behind an 85-yard touchdown run by Eric Penick, a game that propelled Notre Dame to the 1973 national championship. The Irish scored to make it 24–0 just before halftime and kicked off to Anthony Davis. That's when the nightmare began. Davis took the kickoff back for a touchdown. Although the Irish led 24–6 at halftime, the tide had turned. Davis went on to score five more second-half touchdowns and USC stunned Notre Dame 55–24. After each and every Trojan score, "that damn song," the USC fight song, was played. As if to prove Pavlov's theory, it made Irish fans sick each time they heard it. Legend has it that back on the Notre Dame campus, where some students were spending Thanksgiving weekend, television sets flew out of windows as the game turned into a rout.

2. "Green Machine"

The 1977 game went down in Irish lore even before it was played. With the band on the field, a huge Trojan horse was rolled out of the north end zone of Notre Dame Stadium. As the belly of the horse opened, out came three players clad in gold pants and gold helmets, but they were wearing *green,* not the traditional Irish navy blue, jerseys. In what many now refer to as the "Green Jersey Game," Notre Dame routed USC 49–19. Like the 1973 game, it ignited another national championship drive. Green jerseys became a staple the remainder of that season and into future seasons. Gerry Faust even resurrected them in the 1980s for a USC game.

3. *"1988 Showdown"*

The 1988 game was a classic. Number 1 vs. number 2. Both undefeated and squaring off at Notre Dame fans' least favorite venue, the Los Angeles Coliseum. It had been a storybook season to that point for the Irish, but most fans faced this game with some apprehension. After all, the Coliseum had been a house of horrors for Notre Dame over the years. To add to ND's worries, two young running backs, Tony Brooks and Ricky Watters, had been suspended for the game because they had been late for a team meeting.

Irish fears quickly eased as they attacked from the outset. Tony Rice completed a long pass from his end zone when the Trojans had them pinned deep in their own territory. Defensive coordinator Barry Alvarez played a lot of man-to-man coverage to allow his front seven to pressure USC quarterback Rodney Peete.

Right before the half, that strategy turned into six points as Stan Smagala picked off Peete and returned the interception for a touchdown. Peete was leveled on the play. Do you remember by whom? He was originally recruited as a fullback out of Cincinnati, Ohio. But he was tall and ran tall, making him an easy target. Pro scouts always thought he was being played out of position, and Lou Holtz agreed. Holtz moved him to rush end, a position he liked so much, he stayed for a fifth season at ND. Need another hint? He was one of the Three Amigos along with linebackers Wesley Pritchett and Mike Stonebreaker. That's right, Frank Stams, who was in Peete's face all day on the pass rush, took the opportunity of the interception return to flatten Rodney Peete as he was turning to run upfield. Those days at fullback paid off; he had laid the perfect block.

The Irish won 27–10.

4. The Game After the "Game of the Century"

Although today there seems to be a game of the century each week, in 1966 there really was one and it wasn't USC. The 10–10 tie with Michigan State has been the subject of much prose over the years. It was a battle for the ages, where Ara Parseghian was criticized for "playing for the tie." However, because the game was played in East Lansing and because the Irish played with second-string quarterback Coley O'Brien, they were ranked higher in the polls following the MSU tie. This final game of the season was a way to cement the national title for 1966.

Notre Dame certainly did that by routing USC 51–0. Coley O'Brien had a great game substituting for Hanratty. He threw three touchdown passes, including two to Jim Seymour. Notre Dame turned two interceptions into touchdowns to add to the score.

In the Heisman Streak from 1964–1968 three Heisman Trophy winners played in this game. Can you name them? Okay, O. J. Simpson is easy. How about an Irish quarterback and another tailback from tailback U? Right, John Huarte is the quarterback who went from obscurity to stardom under first-year coach Ara Parseghian. But who is that other tailback? Here is a hint: He is still connected with USC. Getting warmer? Here is another hint:

He played with the Kansas City Chiefs in the NFL. Yeah, that's it, Mike Garrett. He won the Heisman Trophy in 1965, played on the Chiefs team that won Super Bowl IV, and is now the USC athletic director.

5. *"The Monsoon Loss"*

In 1970 Notre Dame brought another undefeated squad to Los Angeles and had to endure driving rain and mud. The conditions affected the Irish more than the Trojans, as Notre Dame turned the ball over eight times. USC seemed right at home with the conditions, as they didn't turn the ball over once. Not only that, they recovered two fumbles in the end zone for touchdowns, one of their own and one of Notre Dame's fumbles. Theismann had a marvelous game statistically as he threw for 524 yards on 33 of 58 passing. He, too, had the turnover bug with four interceptions. Final score: USC 38, ND 28.

ND had two great bowl victories against Alabama after the '73 and '74 seasons.
(Photo courtesy of Tony Pace)

Victories

The stories about the great games and great comebacks live on for generations. This chapter will focus on some of the most memorable that always evoke conversation.

I. The first big game. Army versus Notre Dame, November 1, 1913

True or False

1. _____ Army paid Notre Dame $1,000 to travel to West Point to play this game.

2. _____ Quarterback Gus Dorais fumbled on the opening series.

3. _____ Army led at halftime 14–13.

4. _____ After missing on his first two passes, Dorais hit 14 of the next 15 for 243 yards.

5. _____ Dwight Eisenhower was a member of that Army team.

II. "Win one for the Gipper"

The 1928 game against Army was the game Rockne waited for to use his "win one for the Gipper" speech.

True or False

1. _____ Notre Dame never trailed in this game.

2. _____ Reserve end Johnny O'Brien, a hurdler on the track team, scored the winning touchdown on a 32-yard pass from Butch Niemiec.

3. _____ Army was stopped on the one-yard line when the game ended.

4. _____ Notre Dame lost their next two games to finish 5–4; this game helped Rockne avert a losing season.

III. The original Game of the Century

Notre Dame–Ohio State in 1935 is still referred to by many as the game of the century. Now they occur every week. Back then it really meant something.

True or False

1. _____ Starting quarterback Andy Pilney, who rallied Notre Dame from a 12–0 deficit, didn't throw the game-winning touchdown.

2. _____ Notre Dame didn't attempt to kick its extra points but it failed on all three two-point conversion attempts.

3. _____ The ND player who brought in the game-winning play had snuck on the train with the team to the game.

4. _____ Bill Shakespeare threw a pass that was dropped by an OSU defender before he threw the touchdown pass.

IV. Game of the Century II

November 1966. #1 versus #2 in East Lansing, Michigan. It was Ara Parseghian's third season and it would become the most talked-about game of his tenure.

True or False

1. _____ Terry Hanratty didn't even dress for this game.

2. _____ Nick Eddy didn't dress for the game due to a shoulder injury.

3. _____ Notre Dame's only touchdown was a 31-yard pass from Coley O'Brien to Bob Gladieux.

4. _____ Notre Dame had a chance to win after a fourth-quarter Tom Schoen interception, but they turned the ball back to MSU on a Larry Conjar fumble.

Answers

I. The first big game. Army versus Notre Dame, November 1, 1913

1. **True.**

2. **True.**

3. **False.** Notre Dame led by the same score.

4. **True.** It was the dawn of the pass as a weapon in football.

5. **True.** The future general and president may have learned something that day.

II. "Win one for the Gipper"

1. **False.** It was scoreless at halftime and Army scored first in the third quarter.

2. **True.**

3. **True.** The clock ran out on the Cadets.

4. **True.** Rockne never lost another game after this season.

III. The original Game of the Century

1. **True.** He was knocked from the game with a torn knee cartilage.

2. **False.** They just missed these PAT attempts.

3. **True.** Reserve quarterback Jim McKenna didn't even have pads.

4. **True.**

IV. Game of the Century II

1. **False.** He was knocked from the game by Bubba Smith.

2. **True.**

3. **True.**

4. **False.** Joe Azzaro missed a 42-yard field goal after an offensive series that lost six yards.

This is the play that made Rudy famous.
(Photo courtesy of University of Notre Dame)

Walk-ons

Notre Dame gets all the players it wants. There is never any room for unknown players. Hardly true. One even has a movie based on his story. Here's what Rudy had to say about walk-ons:

Walk-ons are dreamers. They believe if they work at it they can make it happen. They believe the goal of being part of the team is worth the effort. If you get to play, well, that's utopia.

— Dan "Rudy" Ruettiger
1975 team

Match Up the Walk-on

1. He kicked for the 1979–80 Irish.   **A.** Mike Brennan

2. A tight end, he also excelled on   **B.** Mike Oriard
special teams for the 1996 squad.

3. This walk-on was a three-time   **C.** Bob Burger
letter winner at fullback from
1993–95.

4. This safety made a key   **D.** Ted Gradel
interception against Purdue in
1995.

5. This walk-on punter has the   **E.** Marcus Thorne
second highest punting average
under Holtz.

6. This center was the only walk-on   **F.** Mark Monahan
to become a captain of a Notre
Dame team.

7. This guard from Cincinnati   **G.** Vince Phelan
started on the 1980 Super Bowl
squad.

8. This walk-on kicker won   **H.** Kevin Carretta
Academic All-American honors.

9. This lacrosse player started at   **I.** Chuck Male
tackle for the 1989 team.

Name the Walk-ons

Many Notre Dame kickers have been walk-ons. Who among the following were walk-ons?

1. Dave Reeve
2. John Carney
3. Kevin Pendergast
4. Hal Von Wyl
5. Harry Oliver

6. Mike Johnston
7. Kevin Kopka
8. Reggie Ho
9. Stefan Schroffner

Matchup
ANSWERS

1. **I**, Chuck Male
2. **H**, Kevin Carretta
3. **E**, Marcus Thorne
4. **F**, Mark Monahan
5. **G**, Vince Phelan

6. **B**, Mike Oriard
7. **C**, Bob Burger
8. **D**, Ted Gradel
9. **A**, Mike Brennan

Name the Walk-ons
ANSWERS

1. No
2. Yes
3. Yes

4. No
5. No
6. Yes

7. No
8. Yes
9. Yes

"Xtras"

by Glen Dansforth

The ND student section on any given Saturday afternoon in the fall *(Photo courtesy of Tony Pace)*

If there is one universal trait shared by fans of the Fighting Irish it's a great sense of humor. This chapter is designed to celebrate that trait and to give readers a break from the stress of trying to answer the questions throughout this book. As the Fighting Irish faithful will immediately recognize, this chapter is written tongue-in-cheek. For the humor impaired (i.e., fans of Penn State, USC, Miami, or Michigan), *the author has provided the correct answer for any of the multiple-choice questions that may have a legitimate answer.*

Xtra's Multiple Choice

1. He didn't have an ounce of talent yet somehow managed to overcome incredible odds to fulfill his dream. His name is:

   A. Dan "Rudy" Ruettiger
   B. Rush Limbaugh
   C. Gerry Faust
   D. Both B and C

2. One of the most famous lines in Notre Dame history was reenacted on film by Ronald Reagan at the height of his mediocre acting career. Reagan uttered the famous words, "win one for _____":

   A. "The Zipper" (Which was the nickname of a former Notre Dame quarterback who had been kicked off the team after being caught with members of the opposing team's cheerleading squad once too often.)
   B. "The Dipper" (The nickname of the defensive end whose love of ice cream proved to be his downfall. Team doctors were forced to suspend him after he tipped the scales at 600 pounds.)
   C. "The Flipper" (The nickname of a promising wide receiver whose career was cut short after taking a shot to the head. Convinced he was a dolphin, "The Flipper" would only play on wet fields.)
   D. "The Gipper" (The Fighting Irish weren't noted for coming up with clever nicknames and usually chose one that was a play on the person's name. "The Gipper" was chosen for George Gipp after the alternative, "The Gimp," was rejected in a precursor to the politically correct movement that would become popular decades later.)

3. Scenario: There were three seconds left in the game. Notre Dame, trailing by six points, had the ball on the 50-yard line. What play was sent in? (HINT: Lou Holtz was the coach at the time.)

   A. Option left
   B. Option right
   C. Allow the quarterback to call an audible after determining what defense he's facing (He's given the choice of option left or option right.)
   D. The "Hail Mary Option" (The quarterback waits until he's about to be tackled, then laterals the ball as far as he can, hoping a teammate can catch it and run 70–80 yards for a touchdown.)

4. The Miami Hurricanes were very successful in the 80s. The main reason for their success was:

   A. The University of Miami's administration voted to remove "literacy" as a requirement for admission to the university.
   B. Due to prison overcrowding, the state of Florida was forced to implement an early-release program for felons.
   C. The potency of illegal drugs tripled.
   D. All of the above.

5. In a slick marketing ploy, Notre Dame quarterback Joe Theismann (pronounced Theez-man) changed the pronunciation of his name to:

   A. Thyshe-man (He hoped it would land him the role of spokesman for Fleischmann's margarine.)
   B. Thice-man (He hoped to make it big in stand-up comedy.)
   C. Thize-man (He knew the only way anyone might as-

sociate him with the Heisman trophy was if he changed his name to rhyme with the award.)

D. Thiemaster (He was thinking infomercial before his time.)

6. Notre Dame found it much more difficult to recruit top talent during the 90s because they couldn't offer the same benefits as many other schools. Which benefit enticed the most recruits from joining the Fighting Irish?

A. An off-shore bank account
B. Trash barrels filled with anabolic steroids
C. A degree in shoelace tying
D. South Bend "snow fests"

7. All but one of the following quotes were made by Lou Holtz. Which one?

A. "Anytime your defense gives up more points than your basketball team, you're in trouble."

B. "My athletes are always willing to accept my advice as long as it doesn't conflict with their views."

C. "Anytime you see one of these preseason magazines, you always see Notre Dame ranked in the top 20 because it sells magazines. If we're any good, they put us in the top three. If they think we're going to be decent, we're in the top six. If they think we have a chance to be pretty good, we're in the top 10. If they don't think we're going to be very good, we're in the top 15. And if they think we're going to be horrendous, we're somewhere between 15 and 20."

D. (When asked about preseason polls that ranked a poor Notre Dame team in the top 20): "I told them the only way they could lose credibility quicker would be to put me in the swimsuit issue."

E. "A lifetime contract for a coach means if you're ahead in the third quarter and moving the ball, they can't fire you."

F. "The expectations here at Notre Dame can change a little bit as you go along. When I first started, everybody said they just wanted us to be competitive. That first season in 1986 we went 5–6 and lost five games by a total of 14 points. But people said, 'No, when we said competitive, we meant we want you to win.' So the next year we went 8–4 and played in a New Year's Day bowl. But they said, 'No, when we said we want you to win, we meant win them all.' So the next year we did win them all. We went 12–0 and won the national championship. But they said, 'No, you don't understand, we meant we want you to win big.' That's the way it goes at Notre Dame."

G. "When students at Notre Dame pay their tuition, they believe that entitles them to one national championship during their four years here."

H. (After Notre Dame upset Florida in the 1992 Sugar Bowl): "I can't wait to get back to the restaurant and see the waiter who said, 'Cherrios and Notre Dame are different: Cheerios belong in a bowl.' " (After the Sugar Bowl, General Mills sent 120 boxes of Cheerios to Holtz with a note saying, "Like the Fighting Irish, we have been one of America's favorites for years. And as your team dramatically proved, both do belong in bowls.")

I. (On taking a part-time job selling cemetery plots after his wife told him he couldn't sell anything): "She was wrong. By the end of the season I'd sold our stereo, our car, her jewels, and our television."

J. (On why he believes linemen are so secure): "They're used to being held all the time."

K. "It didn't bother me that I ranked 234th in my high school graduating class of 273—until I heard the principal say that it was a stupid class."

L. (On whether he agreed with people who said he was the best coach in the country): "Absolutely. There are a thousand better coaches in the cities, but I'm the best in the country."

M. (On Rocket Ismail): "I knew he was fast, but I never knew how fast until I saw him playing tennis with himself."

N. "The best way to save face is by keeping the lower part of it shut."

O. "Sometimes I like to get drunk and mow the lawn wearing only a tutu."

8. What item was Lou Holtz asked to kiss in order to ensure good luck for Notre Dame football?

   A. Pamela Lee Anderson
   B. The Blarney Stone
   C. Richard Simmons
   D. All of the below

9. In order to have any hope of matching the success of the football program, the Notre Dame basketball program must mimic the football team's traditions. What is the first thing they must do?

   A. Have players shave their heads and paint them gold
   B. Obtain a giant painting of "Three-pointer Jesus"
   C. Hire Lou Holtz as head coach (Who cares if the offense is dull and predictable if they win games?)
   D. Win several national championships

10. Who is the person famous for turning the pass into an art form?

    A. Knute Rockne
    B. Rudolph Valentino
    C. Bill Clinton
    D. All of the above

11. Name the Four Horsemen:

    A. Moe, Larry, Curly, and Shemp
    B. Harry Stuhldreher, Jim Crowley, Don Miller, and Elmer Layden
    C. Wilt Chamberlain, Milton Berle, Warren Beatty, and Bill Clinton
    D. John, Paul, George, and Ringo

12. Which of the following was not one of Knute Rockne's famous halftime pep talks?

    A. (As Notre Dame was ready to return to the field after an embarrassing first half): "Let's go, ladies."
    B. "Win one for the Gipper."
    C. (Upon entering the locker room where the football team sat following a terrible first half): "Oh, I'm sorry. I thought this was the Notre Dame locker room."
    D. "If we beat the spread, the beer is on me."

13. Only one of the following is not a work of fiction. Which one is it?

    A. *Moby Dick*
    B. *Under the Tarnished Dome*
    C. *Tom Sawyer*
    D. *Webster's Dictionary*

14. What was the nickname of Raghib Ismail?

    A. "That really fast guy"
    B. "Rocket"
    C. "Zippy"
    D. "Old Blue Eyes"

15. Which of the following is not associated with Knute Rockne:

    A. The buttonhook
    B. The use of the forward pass
    C. "Win one for the Gipper"
    D. The use of Whoopee Cushions to express disagreement with an official's call

16. Which of the following books is most likely to make it to bookstores in the new future:

    A. *How to Win Friends and Influence People,* by Steve Spurrier
    B. *Why the Run and Shoot Offense Is Vastly Underrated,* by Lou Holtz
    C. *Just Say No,* by Barry Switzer
    D. *How to Steal a National Championship from Notre Dame,* by Bobby Bowden

17. Which of the following Notre Dame–related quotes was never spoken?

    A. Beano Cook said that there are two things one should never bet against, "Russia in the winter, and Notre Dame in South Bend."
    B. Notre Dame tackle Tim Marshall, surprised to be named to the 1983 All-American team after he was sidelined for the entire 1982 season with an injury,

said, "If I sit out another year I'll probably get the Heisman Trophy."

C. Mike Stonebreaker said, "We believe in the spirit of Notre Dame, but some people think it's false. I understand their point. If we're so blessed then why did we go 5–6 in 1985?"

D. Knute Rockne said, "I found prayers work best when you have big players."

E. When asked what it was like touring Brazil, former Marquette player Jerome Whitehead said, "We had 25,000 people booing us and throwing garbage on our heads. It was like the whole country was Notre Dame."

F. Former Miami Hurricanes coach Jimmy Johnson said, "Notre Dame is the greatest school and football program in history. The University of Miami is Pop Warner in comparison. We don't belong on the planet, never mind the same field, as the Fighting Irish."

Xtras
ANSWERS

1. **D:** Unlike Faust and Limbaugh, Dan Ruettiger, whose heroic struggle was immortalized in the film *Rudy,* possessed a lot of talent.

2. **D:** "The Gipper."

5. **C:** Thize-man.

7. **O:** "Sometimes I like to get drunk and mow the lawn wearing only a tutu."

8. **B:** The Blarney Stone.

11. **B:** Harry Stuhldreher, Jim Crowley, Don Miller, and Elmer Layden.

12. **D:** "If we beat the spread, the beer is on me."

14. **B:** "Rocket."

15. **D:** The use of Whoopee Cushions to express disagreement with an official's call.

17. **F:** As hard as it is to believe, there is no record of former Miami Hurricanes coach Jimmy Johnson ever saying, "Notre Dame is the greatest school and football program in history. The University of Miami is Pop Warner in comparison. We don't belong on the planet, never mind the same field, as the Fighting Irish."

Questions Complete with Answers

1. What is the penalty if a Notre Dame player is flagged for a personal foul:
   A: Three "Our Fathers" and twelve "Hail Marys."

2. Steve Young served as the backup for the most famous Notre Dame alumnus (Joe Montana) during the 80s. Who serves as the backup for the most famous Notre Dame alumnus during the 90s?
   A: Kathy Lee Gifford.

3. If a top player from Penn State wants to transfer to Notre Dame, what is the only position he must play if he hopes to ever see any action?
   A: Hunchback.

4. What is enormous, filled with hot air, and is frequently seen at stadiums during the college football game of the week?
A: Keith Jackson

5. If Knute Rockne were alive today, what would cause him the most grief?
A: The people who would inevitably introduce him by the last name of Gingrich.

6. Because Notre Dame's cheerleading squad is coed, what ideal nickname for the squad cannot be used?
A: The Flying Nuns.

7. What was Notre Dame's greatest acquisition ever?
A: Their own network.

8. What is the reason for Notre Dame's incredible rivalry with USC?
A: Catholics are afraid they might go to hell unless they destroy the Trojans.

9. When football fans hear the term "The Golden Dome," what do they automatically think of?
A: Terry Bradshaw's head.

10. The Notre Dame fight song was written after the original fight song failed to arouse fan spirit. What was the original team fight song?
A: Bringing in the Sheep.

11. What is the main reason Notre Dame doesn't have the greatest college football program?
A: The correct answer to this question would include any of the following: Excuse Me?; This better be a joke, humor boy!; or any violent reaction, up to and including throwing this book through a plate-glass window. (If you harm this book, points will be deducted.)

12. Name the year in which Notre Dame broke down and finally allowed the ultimate weapon in enticing top recruits to the university?

A: 1972 (when the college finally began admitting women).

Yardage

Football yields plenty of statistics, but the game is most often decided by turnovers and a few key plays. Nonetheless there are some interesting tidbits in the yardage statistics.

Multiple Choice

1. Which Notre Dame Heisman Trophy winner had the most career passing yards?

   A. Angelo Bertelli
   B. Johnny Lujack
   C. Paul Hornung
   D. John Huarte

2. Which Notre Dame Heisman Trophy winner had the most passing yards in one season?

   A. Angelo Bertelli
   B. John Lujack
   C. Paul Hornung
   D. John Huarte

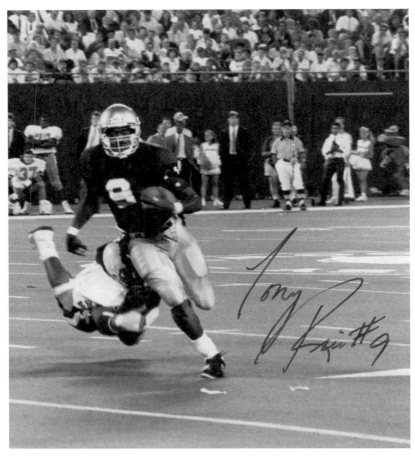

Tony Rice ran for the most yards of any modern quarterback at Notre Dame.
(Photo by Neal P. Kemp)

3. Since 1950, Notre Dame's defense has ranked #1 nationally in terms of yardage allowed only once. What year was it?

   A. 1964
   B. 1966
   C. 1974
   D. 1980

4. Which receiver amassed the most career yardage?

   A. Tom Gatewood
   B. Jim Seymour
   C. Tim Brown
   D. Derrick Mayes

5. Who has the most career punting yards for Notre Dame?

   A. Craig Hentrich
   B. Joe Restic
   C. Blair Kiel
   D. Brian Doherty

6. What is the Notre Dame team record for most total offensive yards in one game?

   A. 570
   B. 631
   C. 701
   D. 720

7. Under which coach did Notre Dame amass its greatest rushing yards in one game?

   A. Rockne
   B. Anderson
   C. Layden

D. Leahy
E. Brennan
F. Parseghian
G. Devine
H. Faust
I. Holtz

8. The Notre Dame defense has held many teams to negative passing yardage. When was the last year that happened and who was the opponent?

   A. Georgia—Sugar Bowl 1981
   B. Alabama—1980
   C. Navy—1988
   D. Georgia Tech—1976

9. Who holds the record for total yardage in a season (rushing, passing, receiving, and returns)?

   A. Joe Theismann
   B. Allen Pinkett
   C. Rick Mirer
   D. Tony Rice

10. Who holds the career record for total yardage?

   A. Joe Theismann
   B. Allen Pinkett
   C. Rick Mirer
   D. Tony Rice

Multiple Choice
ANSWERS

1. **A:** The "Springfield Rifle" had 2,578 yards passing.

2. **D:** Huarte didn't play much until his senior season; he completed 2,062 yards passing.

3. **C:** Despite the season-ending rout at USC, Ara's last team was unsurpassed in terms of yardage surrendered.

4. **D:** Mayes outdistanced all of them with 2,512 yards.

5. **C:** With 10,534 yards, Kiel had more than 2,000 yards on his nearest competitor.

6. **D:** Notre Dame had 720 yards of total offense versus Navy in 1969.

7. **B:** The year that Rockne died, his former chargers ran over Drake with 629 yards. Hunk Anderson was in Rockne's old position.

8. **D.**

9. **A:** Theismann had 2,820 in 1970.

10. **C:** Mirer led the potent Notre Dame offense to 6,907 yards.

Ziggy Czarobski

Ziggy has been called "The Clown Prince of Notre Dame Football," so many times you would think it's part of his name. To say he was a character is an understatement. As his legend has grown over time, the tales have gotten even taller. That makes fact-finding a bit difficult, but here goes.

Multiple Choice

1. How many games did Notre Dame lose in Ziggy's junior and senior season?

   A. Three
   B. Two
   C. One
   D. Zero

2. How many national championships did Notre Dame win while Ziggy was on the squad?

   A. One
   B. Two
   C. Three
   D. Four

3. When Ziggy played tackle in 1942 he was listed at 205 pounds. How much heavier was he five seasons later after serving in the Armed Forces?

   A. Same weight
   B. Eight pounds
   C. Thirteen pounds
   D. Twenty pounds

4. What was Ziggy's uniform number?

   A. 60
   B. 66
   C. 76
   D. 79

5. In the annual team photo, Notre Dame football players usually sit with the seniors closest to the camera and then descend by rows with the coaches in back. What row did Ziggy sit in as a senior?

   A. First row
   B. Second row
   C. Third row
   D. Back row

6. Who drafted Ziggy?

   A. Cleveland Browns
   B. Detroit Lions
   C. Chicago Bears
   D. Chicago Cardinals

7. What city did Ziggy play professional football in?

   A. St. Louis
   B. Chicago

C. Detroit

D. Los Angeles

Multiple Choice
ANSWERS

1. **D:** Seventeen wins and one tie, the famous 0–0 standoff with Army in 1946.

2. **C:** 1943 and 1946 and 1947. Only Ziggy and his teammates from those years can claim that fact.

3. **B:** All that maturation and only eight pounds.

4. **C:** Worn proudly, too!

5. **D:** Where else would he have sat!

6. **D:** But he never played for them.

7. **B:** Ziggy went back to his roots and played for the two successive All-American Football Conference teams in Chicago: The Rockets and the Hornets.

FINAL WORD

As we head into the 1997 season we are curious about the new stories that will emerge, the new records that will be set, and the new personalities that will break through.

Some educated guesses:

If Ron Powlus remains healthy, he could set many new passing records; Allen Rossum may surpass Tim Brown as the most prolific scorer on punt returns; and watch out for Autry Denson coming off a 1,000-yard season, as he still has two seasons of eligibility remaining.

We had no idea when we started this project that 1996 would be Lou Holtz's final season in South Bend. Although we are sorry to see him go, this book comes at an appropriate time: the start of the Bob Davie era. We obviously hope this new era is more like those of Holtz or Parseghian than Brennan or Faust.

By the way, the answer to that question from the introduction is that Pace picked Texas to win by one in the 1978 Cotton Bowl. And you thought Jim Samson got grief after missing the final extra point against USC in November. Thank God there wasn't E-mail back then.

We hope you enjoyed the book. Maybe we'll do an updated version after Notre Dame wins its next national championship!